Language Policy and the Future of Europe

This volume offers an insider perspective on language policy in the EU, bringing together two key figures well acquainted with its development to reflect critically on the future of language policy and practices in post-Brexit Europe.

Born out of Alice Leal's *English and translation in the European Union*, this volume features annotated interviews with Seán Ó Riain, newly appointed Multilingualism Officer by the Irish diplomatic service, whose decades of experience in key milestones in EU language policy offer a unique perspective on its development. Each chapter, bookended by a contextual introduction and a closing commentary by Leal, addresses such key questions as: How long can the EU keep linguistic and cultural spheres off the policy-making agenda? How has the ECRML impacted linguistic diversity in the region? How widespread is the dominance of English in EU institutions today and what impact does it have on EU multilingualism? Why is EU language policy not given the attention it warrants? What does the future of language policy hold in this post-Brexit era?

Providing exclusive insights into EU language policy, this book will appeal to scholars in applied linguistics, translation studies, sociolinguistics, and political science, as well as stakeholders in language policy and planning.

Alice Leal is Associate Professor of Translation and Interpreting Studies at the University of the Witwatersrand, South Africa.

Seán Ó Riain is an Irish diplomat and linguist with over 40 years of diplomatic service, presently in charge of the promotion of multilingualism at the Irish Foreign Ministry.

Routledge Focus on Applied Linguistics

Contesting Grand Narratives of the Intercultural
Adrian Holliday

Sustainability of Blended Language Learning Programs
Technology Integration in English for Academic Purposes
Cynthia Nicholas Palikat and Paul Gruba

Discourses of Borders and the Nation
A Discourse-Historical Analysis
Massimiliano Demata

Health Disparities and the Applied Linguist
Maricel G. Santos, Rachel Showstack, Glenn Martínez, Drew Colcher, Dalia Magaña

Instruction Giving in Online Language Lessons
A Multimodal (Inter)action Analysis
Müge Satar and Ciara R. Wigham

Language Policy and the Future of Europe
A Conversation with Seán Ó Riain
Alice Leal and Seán Ó Riain

For more information about this series, please visit: www.routledge.com/Routledge-Focus-on-Applied-Linguistics/book-series/RFAL

Language Policy and the Future of Europe
A Conversation with Seán Ó Riain

Alice Leal and Seán Ó Riain

NEW YORK AND LONDON

First published 2023
by Routledge
605 Third Avenue, New York, NY 10158

and by Routledge
4 Park Square, Milton Park, Abingdon, Oxon, OX14 4RN

Routledge is an imprint of the Taylor & Francis Group, an informa business

© 2023 Alice Leal and Seán Ó Riain

The right of Alice Leal and Seán Ó Riain to be identified as authors of this work has been asserted in accordance with sections 77 and 78 of the Copyright, Designs and Patents Act 1988.

All rights reserved. No part of this book may be reprinted or reproduced or utilised in any form or by any electronic, mechanical, or other means, now known or hereafter invented, including photocopying and recording, or in any information storage or retrieval system, without permission in writing from the publishers.

Trademark notice: Product or corporate names may be trademarks or registered trademarks and are used only for identification and explanation without intent to infringe.

Library of Congress Cataloging-in-Publication Data
Names: Leal, Alice, author, interviewer. |
Ó Riain, Seán, 1955– author, interviewee.
Title: Language policy and the future of Europe : a conversation with Seán Ó Riain / Alice Leal, Seán Ó Riain.
Description: First edition. | New York, NY : Routledge, 2024. |
Series: Routledge focus on applied linguistics |
Includes bibliographical references and index.
Identifiers: LCCN 2023009567 | ISBN 9781032378145 (hardback) |
ISBN 9781032378152 (paperback) | ISBN 9781003342069 (ebook)
Subjects: LCSH: Language policy–European Union countries. |
Multilingualism–Political aspects–European Union countries. |
European Union countries–Languages–Political aspects. | Ó Riain, Seán, 1955–
Interviews. | LCGFT: Discursive works. | Interviews.
Classification: LCC P119.32.E85 L48 2024 | DDC 306.44/94–dc23/eng/20230313
LC record available at https://lccn.loc.gov/2023009567

ISBN: 978-1-032-37814-5 (hbk)
ISBN: 978-1-032-37815-2 (pbk)
ISBN: 978-1-003-34206-9 (ebk)

DOI: 10.4324/9781003342069

Typeset in Times New Roman
by Newgen Publishing UK

Contents

Preface vii
Introduction xiii

1 The European Charter for Regional or Minority Languages 1

2 The status of multilingualism in the European Commission 31

3 The European Commission and English as a "lingua franca" 57

4 Migrant and non-territorial languages in the EU 92

5 Language policy and official EU status 109

6 Ireland and multilingualism in a post-Brexit EU 129

Conclusions 146

Index *150*

Preface

When Professor Alice Leal walked into my office at the Irish Embassy in Vienna in 2021, I had little idea that our meeting would lead to this book. She had asked for an interview concerning my activities in the language policy area. As we spoke the topics grew and grew, and led to related discussions, until we both realised that we had the material for a book. It was immediately apparent that we shared a passionate interest in language policy, translation and language diversity. As I read Alice Leal's inspiring work *English and translation in the European Union*, I began to see many exciting possibilities for our future cooperation in raising awareness of the importance of linguistic diversity.

I am a diplomat who has had the privilege of representing Ireland in six countries (Austria, Australia, Poland, Germany, Belgium/EU and Argentina) and at various international organisations (European Union, United Nations, Council of Europe). My PhD, from Trinity College Dublin, supervised by Professor Máirtín Ó Murchú, is on language planning in Ireland and Québec. I have achieved fluency in eight languages, can read another five, and language policy and planning has been one of the major passions of my life. In 2007–2015 I headed the fledgling Irish language web translation section at the European Commission's Directorate-General for Translation (DGT), and was in charge of the Irish, French and German sections of the website of Ireland's presidency of the EU Council in 2013. My wife, Natalie, is French and we speak French together. My two adult daughters, Aisling and Ciara, are native speakers of Irish (and French). At present I work as the first ever Multilingualism Officer at the Irish Foreign Ministry, with a mission to increase the motivation of all Irish diplomatic colleagues to learn and use other languages.

What was the origin of this passion for languages and language policy? I grew up in Tipperary, in the south of Ireland, in an area that had lost the Irish language within living memory. My father, who spoke no Irish, remembered his grandfather, who was a native speaker of the language. For non-Irish readers, Irish, sometimes inaccurately referred to as Gaelic, is as distant from English as Polish is from German. My father spoke only English, but it was an English peppered with Irish words (over 400 of them) and, more importantly, Irish syntax and phonology. Attending primary school, some other pupils and I were physically punished as our English was considered "too Irish'."

To give one example: Irish has a habitual present tense of the verb "to be," paralleled to similar forms in Polish and other Slavic languages, but which is lacking in standard English. Irish distinguishes *bíonn sí anseo go minic* (she is often here, Polish *ona często bywa tutaj*) from *tá sí anseo anois* (she is here now, Polish *ona jest tutaj teraz*). The lack of this tense in standard English led to the creation of *I do be, she does be* in Hiberno-English. Such forms were in universal use in the English of the area where I grew up. As a four-year-old beginning school, when I was slapped for speaking like this, I innocently asked why. The answer: "Children in England do not speak like that, it's incorrect." To which I replied, "But I am not an English child." The question of language and identity was already central to my being.

My upbringing was unusual in the area in that my mother spoke Irish fluently, as she had learned all subjects through Irish at school. She regularly spoke Irish to us, so that we were bilingual before beginning school. This was an educational advantage, as most other children spoke only English. Language fascinated me from an early age, and I collected in a copybook the 400 Irish words my father used in English – words understood and used by everybody of his generation. As a teenager I was taken by the beauty of Irish language literature, particularly by its song, poetry and proverbs. Irish became a literary language in 597 AD, one of the first in Europe, after Latin and Ancient Greek. My wish to deepen my knowledge of Irish continued to grow. Though taught through English at secondary school, I decided to do my entire Leaving Certificate (Baccalaureate) examination through Irish – even my mother thought this was taking it too far! I relished the extra work, however, and the extent to which it developed my Irish.

In addition, I began to study other Celtic languages, such as Welsh and Scottish Gaelic. The survival of Irish during all the centuries of foreign occupation, and the constant attempts of the colonial administration to suppress it, was a further incentive to study it. The first laws against the use of Irish, the Statutes of Kilkenny of 1366, were aimed mainly at preventing the assimilation of the English colony in Ireland to Irish culture. So unsuccessful were these laws that, in 1541, when the English King Henry VIII decided to appoint himself king of Ireland, the official proclamation had to be translated into Irish to be understood by the English colonial parliament in Dublin. Irish remained the majority language of Ireland until the Great Famine of the mid-nineteenth century, and the movement set up to prevent its disappearance was one of the main factors leading to Irish political independence in 1922. Even a non-Irish speaker like my father was proud to see his children speaking Irish together – in his words, "It is proof conclusive of the failure of the conquest."

At university in Galway, I met many kindred spirits and inspiring professors. My initial degree was in Irish and French, with German as a subsidiary subject and one year of Welsh. Two very intensive courses in Aberystwyth brought my Welsh to fluency, and a course in Stornoway gave me a good grounding in Scottish Gaelic. My MA in linguistics, supervised by Professor Gearóid Mac Eoin, dealt with the evolution of verbal aspects from the Old Irish of the seventh century to the modern language. I became friendly with native speakers of all three main dialects of Irish, and shared a house with four of them, which became a mini-*Gaeltacht*, or Irish-speaking area. A book based on my PhD thesis, *Pleanáil Teanga in Éirinn 1919–1985* (Language Planning in Ireland), was published by the then *Bord na Gaeilge*, the state agency for the promotion of the Irish language. It features on the reading lists of many third-level courses of Irish, particularly the increasing number which focus on language planning.

On joining the Foreign Ministry my first diplomatic posting was to Vienna. We organised a three-month seminar on Austria's Celtic past, bringing lecturers and performers from Ireland, leading to the screening of Frank Delaney series *The Celts* on Austrian television. On returning to Ireland, I joined the Council of Europe Section and represented Ireland on the intergovernmental committee, which drew up the European Charter on Regional and

Minority Languages. I also became secretary of the Irish national committee of the European Bureau for Less-Used Languages, EBLUL.[1] During my posting to Australia I ran a weekly Irish language class which attracted over 40 young Australians, not all of them of Irish descent. On my posting to Poland, I supported Irish and Celtic studies at the universities of Poznan and Lublin. While posted to Germany, I was active in the attempt to save Celtic Studies at the Humboldt University, Berlin, and gave many lectures on Irish and Celtic topics.

While a seconded national expert to the European Commission's DGT, I produced some 13,000 web pages in Irish, and trained seven graduates who worked with me as *stagiaires*. I spoke about the Irish language at many conferences organised by the Commission. In addition, I was re-seconded to the Department of the *Taoiseach* (Prime Minister) to take charge of the Irish, French and German sections of the website of Ireland's presidency of the EU Council in 2013 – I produced a further 3,000 web pages in Irish. Over the years I have also studied the Hebrew language revival and have given talks on any possible lessons it may contain for the future of Irish.

The foregoing may help show that my interest in language diversity, particularly in fostering the Irish language, is strong, longstanding and genuine. I now turn to an aspect which may appear controversial, and even contradictory to some – my interest in the international language Esperanto. In an increasingly globalised world, the need for communication on a planetary scale is felt more and more. The void has been filled by ubiquitous English, but I see this as problematic in many respects.

- First, it has been allowed to happen without any scholarly consideration of its possible consequences for other languages.
- Second, the unchecked spread of English is a growing threat to linguistic diversity.
- Third, it gives an unearned and lifelong advantage to the 6 per cent who are native speakers of English over the other 94 per cent of humanity.
- Fourth, only those with a particular talent for learning languages, or the money to spend years in English-speaking countries, can hope to master the language. Some can, therefore, justifiably see the spread of English as hierarchical and undemocratic.

- Fifth, the time and effort needed to master the complexity of English leaves the average student with less time for the study of other languages.
- Sixth, turning to the EU, the growing use of English only within the EU institutions risks making European integration more remote from European citizens – since Brexit only 1 per cent of them have English as their mother tongue.
- Finally, the only comparison of achievement in language learning through objective testing, the European Commission's SurveyLang of 2012, was only conducted up to the B2 level – when I asked the Commission why, the reply was that the number of those who reach C1 level, even in their first foreign language, is of the order of 1 per cent, which is statistically insignificant. The present situation is clearly unsatisfactory, and merits greater attention.

The initial appearance of English being easy to learn is deceptive. True, English is less inflected than many other languages, and does not have the complex tonal system of Chinese. It has, however, several other challenging aspects. In addition to the illogical spelling system, the unpredictability of stress, the complexity of phrasal verbs and parallel vocabulary absorbed from other languages adds to the learning burden. For instance, English has *regal, royal* and *kingly* where most languages have one adjective. I would stress that my opposition is to the dominance of any national language, and not merely to the dominance of English. I see English as a red rose, a beautiful and very popular flower, but how many would like to have a garden full of red roses, with no other flower? That, unfortunately, is where the unchecked spread of English leads, in my view.

Any broad argument in favour of Esperanto would be beyond the scope of this book, but it should be noted that the language is more used than many realise: the Esperanto Wikipedia contains over 330,000 articles, which is more than 11 of the EU's 24 official languages.[2] One aspect, in particular, is worth considering: the propaedeutical approach, i.e., the use of short courses in Esperanto with the aim of accelerating and improving language learning in general. It is noteworthy that the most popular proposal in the cultural and educational area at the recent Conference on the future of Europe was "The EU needs improved language learning."

This was also the fifth most popular of the over 16,000 proposals received from citizens by the Conference. A recent scientific report to the European Parliament, "The European Union's approach to multilingualism in its own communication policy," highlights this fact, stressing an important point that is often overlooked: "There is no common language in the EU spoken at a very good level by the majority of the population." The linguistic consequences of Brexit add to the complexity.

Given this situation, a more in-depth, evidence-based, consideration of the EU's impact on European multilingualism is overdue. The repercussions of EU language policy go far beyond the linguistic area. It has implications for the relationship between the citizen and European integration and may even have a word to say in one of the most important challenges now facing Europe: how to secure peace based on justice on our continent.

Seán Ó Riain[3]
Brussels, 7 February 2023

Notes

1 There has been some controversy surrounding the name of the bureau, which is more commonly known as the "European Bureau of Lesser-Used Languages." We have chosen the more grammatical "less-used" languages.
2 See https://meta.wikimedia.org/wiki/List_of_Wikipedias (last accessed in February 2023).
3 Any opinions expressed by me are personal, and do not commit the Irish Government or its Department of Foreign Affairs to any course of action.

Introduction

In late 2017, I received an invitation from Routledge to write a book manuscript on language policy in the European Union (EU). The book, *English and translation in the European Union*, came out in 2021 and was welcomed by the University of Vienna in 2022 as my *Habilitationsschrift*. Given its transdisciplinarity, the book took me on an inspiring journey through applied and sociolinguistics, philosophy of language and political philosophy, translation studies and political theory, in addition to adjacent disciplines. Despite the fact that my focus lay on the epistemological and normative aspects of the phenomena of EU multilingualism and English as a lingua franca, it soon became clear that I needed to speak to peers in EU institutions and bodies to add a more – albeit limited – practical dimension to the book.

It was Paul Kaye, former language officer at the now defunct European Commission Representation in the UK, who suggested I contact Seán Ó Riain, who at the time was acting Irish Ambassador in Vienna. Our first talk, in a quiet Indian restaurant in the first district in Vienna, flew past. It felt like an immense privilege to be able to sit down with one of my interviewees as the world was grappling with Covid-19. Out of the dozens of EU staff with whom I had contact while researching the book, I only met Ó Riain and Claudia Kropf (from the European Commission Representation in Austria and a translator at the Directorate-General for Translation – DGT) face to face; all other exchanges took place by email and/or through Skype or Zoom.

Among my interlocutors at EU institutions, Ó Riain stood out due to his sharp understanding of and captivating passion for languages and multilingualism. What truly impressed me were the insider stories he had about key moments in the history of multilingualism in Europe, such as the drafting of the European Charter for Regional or Minority Languages (ECRML) and the inclusion of Irish as an official EU language. His input made me wish I could expand my 2021 book in several directions – more background information on the ECRML, on planned languages, on linguistic injustices, on Irish. As my wordcount was already going through the roof, we agreed to work on a new book together – the one you are looking at right now.

Having had a few conversations and many email exchanges with Ó Riain previously, I had a good idea of the realms to which he could contribute most before I first walked into his office in central Vienna in July 2021. I compiled the 15 questions the reader finds in this book, which he agreed were relevant and encapsulated his expertise and experience in language policy. The choice of topics also reflected what I perceived, after extensive research in this field, as relevant areas on which to write a new book: the ECRML (past, present and future), the hierarchy among the languages spoken in the EU, the role of English as the bloc's lingua franca of sorts in the aftermath of the UK's withdrawal from the EU, the revitalisation of Irish vis-à-vis the then upcoming end of the derogation period in which it had been placed by the EU in 2007, the creation of Ó Riain's new post as Multilingualism Officer by the Irish Ministry of Foreign Affairs (which took place while we were conducting the interviews), as well as the work dynamics and the language ideologies of the current custodians of multilingualism in the EU – namely DGT.

The interviews took place in his office, as already noted, in the Irish Embassy in Vienna, on the buzzy Rotenturmstraße, in three sessions between 21 and 30 July 2021. He was aware of the questions that were going to be asked, but his answers were spontaneous, following a thoroughly oral style. I recorded our exchanges using the app Otter, which generated nine audio files totalling 230'18", along with live transcriptions of the dialogue. Our anonymous peer-reviewers – to whom we are thankful for helping us improve this book – later suggested adjusting the transcriptions to conform to a more written style to avoid repetition, which we did. As the reader will see in what follows, the responses were given in monologue style, with the few interruptions by me signalled between square brackets.

The questions were grouped in six clusters of topics, which constitute the chapters that make up this book. Chapter 1, which

Introduction xv

comprises interview questions 1 to 3, revolves around the ECRML and contains exclusive, insider information on the drafting process of the Charter. Questions 4 and 5 make up Chapter 2, which taps into Ó Riain's eight-year experience inside DGT and offers an overview of multilingualism in the Commission. The longest chapter is Chapter 3, which encompasses questions 6 to 8 and is dedicated to the role of the English language in the EU in the wake of Brexit. Chapter 4 includes questions 9 to 10 and is devoted to the urgent issue of EU migrant and non-territorial languages. Questions 11 and 12 are combined in Chapter 5 and shed light on EU language policy through the perspective of official EU status. Finally, Chapter 6, which covers questions 13 to 15, is about the linguistic and diplomatic landscape of post-Brexit Ireland and the creation of Ó Riain's post as Ireland's Multilingualism Officer.

All chapters feature the same tripartite structure, namely introductory remarks on the topics covered in the interview, the interview itself, followed by commentary. This introduction, along with all introductory remarks and commentaries were written by me (Leal), whereas the preface and obviously the interview answers were authored by Ó Riain. We wrote the Final Remarks together. Though there is some cross-referencing across the chapters, we did our best to keep them independent of each other, so that readers can choose the clusters of topics which interest them most. However, reading the book from cover to cover will undoubtedly offer a more congruent picture, as these topics are ineluctably intertwined.

Our main objective with this volume, as we have already signalled, is to gather Ó Riain's insider information, insights and experiences with EU multilingualism. The aim of each chapter's introductory remarks is to situate readers in the cluster of topics in question, including not only background information but also input from scholarly research. Similarly, the commentaries offer a critical appraisal of the content of the interviews very much grounded in academic research. By bringing together a diplomat and an academic, we hope to bridge the gap between academia and decision and policy-making, and welcome further initiatives that follow this line. Since the beginning of our dialogue over 18 months ago, Ó Riain's practical experiences as Multilingualism Officer have flown into Leal's academic research, not least by helping test the language, translation and transcultural turns she proposes for the EU. By the same token, the exchanges with Leal have contributed to Ó Riain's planning to reach the objectives set in his new post.

Beyond these objectives, Ó Riain and Leal are committed to protecting and fostering both individual and societal multilingualism in the EU – and the world, given that Leal has been based in South America, Europe and now Africa, whereas Ó Riain has been posted to Europe, Australia and South America. Despite the different perspectives of the two authors (which will become apparent in what follows), this volume represents another step they undertake – this time together – to raise awareness of the value and importance of multilingualism as the EU stands at a crossroads in the aftermath of the coronavirus pandemic and the invasion of Ukraine. As the reader may have noticed, the Conference on the future of Europe inspired the title of this volume, which brings together a look into the past and present of language policy in the EU, while looking ahead to the future.

Johannesburg, 19 January 2023.

1 The European Charter for Regional or Minority Languages

Introductory remarks

The European Charter for Regional or Minority Languages (ECRML) constitutes one of the key developments in Europe's history to address its multilingualism. The interview with Ó Riain below offers an overview of the drafting process of the ECRML; the main challenges faced; the stance of key participating states; the strategies used to overcome the greatest hurdles; the reasons behind some countries' reluctance to sign and/or ratify the Charter, as well as the outlook for the ECRML in years to come (see Table 1.1).

Originally, the ECRML was an initiative by the Council of Europe (CoE). As outlined by Ó Riain in what follows, the conversations among the then 23 members of the CoE, which culminated in the Charter, had begun in the 1980s. The Standing Conference of Local and Regional Authorities of Europe put forward an initial draft of the Charter. Between 1988 and 1992, the newly formed intergovernmental *Comité Ad Hoc pour les Langues Régionales* (CAHLR), comprising experts from the then 23 CoE member states plus a representative from the Bureau of Less-Used Languages, turned this initial draft into the Charter as we know it today. Having been approved by the CAHLR experts as a convention – as opposed to a recommendation – on 25 June 1992, it was officially adopted by the Committee of Ministers of the CoE. On 5 November 1992, it was opened for signature in Strasbourg, though it did not enter into force until 1 March 1998. This was due to Article 19(1), which stipulates that the Charter may only enter into force three months after at least five

DOI: 10.4324/9781003342069-1

Table 1.1 Council of Europe: Member states by year of accession

Members that participated in to the ECRML talks	**Founding members (May 1949)**	BELGIUM, DENMARK, FRANCE, IRELAND, ITALY, LUXEMBOURG, NETHERLANDS, NORWAY, SWEDEN, UNITED KINGDOM
	August 1949	GREECE, REPUBLIC OF TÜRKIYE
	1950	ICELAND, GERMANY
	1956	AUSTRIA
	1961	CYPRUS
	1963	SWITZERLAND
	1965	MALTA
	1976	PORTUGAL
	1977	SPAIN
	1978	LIECHTENSTEIN
	1988	SAN MARINO
	1989	FINLAND
	1990	HUNGARY
	1991	POLAND
	1992	BULGARIA
Members that joined during / after the ECRML talks	1993	ESTONIA, LITHUANIA, SLOVENIA, THE CZECH REPUBLIC, SLOVAKIA, ROMANIA
	1994	ANDORRA
	1995	LATVIA, ALBANIA, MOLDOVA, UKRAINE, "THE FORMER YUGOSLAV REPUBLIC OF MACEDONIA"
	1996	CROATIA
	1999	GEORGIA
	2001	ARMENIA, AZERBAIJAN
	2002	BOSNIA AND HERZEGOVINA
	2003	SERBIA
	2004	MONACO
	2007	MONTENEGRO
	Applicant country: BELARUS	
	Belarus' special guest status has been suspended due to its lack of respect for human rights and democratic principles.	
	Observers: THE HOLY SEE, THE UNITED STATES, CANADA, JAPAN, MEXICO	

Source: www.coe.int/en/web/tbilisi/the-coe/objectives-and-missions

CoE member states have ratified it. The first states to do so were Norway (1993), Finland (1994), Hungary (1995), Netherlands (1996) and Croatia (1997).

The Charter defines "minority languages" as languages "traditionally used within a given territory of a State by nationals of that State who form a group numerically smaller than the rest of the State's population" and "different from the official language(s) of the State" – see Article 1(a). The adverb "traditionally" is crucial here, as we will see in what follows. Ó Riain stresses the relevance of so-called "autochthonous" languages in the conversations leading up to the ECRML, i.e., languages "indigenous" to a particular territory. Although no set number of years was discussed, the ECRML operates with a notion of languages "historically" (another buzzword in the Charter) spoken in Europe, thus excluding the languages of "recent" migrants – however many decades "recent" implies. In fact, "the languages of migrants" are explicitly excluded in Article 1(a).

In principle, the ECRML also excludes non-territorial languages, as some territorial basis is a pre-requisite for its application. It does, nevertheless, encourage member states to accommodate non-territorial languages as far as possible – see Article 7(5). Romani, for instance, enjoys some protections in 16 countries, as do different Sámi languages in Finland, Norway and Sweden. Sign languages are not contemplated by the ECRML. Despite the suggested definitions of minority languages, the ECRML gives member states free rein to decide which languages qualify as such in their territory.

The ECRML consists of 68 measures aimed at protecting the languages nominated by the member state in question. They are distributed across seven articles or areas, as shown in Table 1.2. Signing the Charter is a largely symbolic step, as it merely implies that the state in question is willing to comply with the general principles of the Charter, stipulated in Article 7, as follows:

> Recognition of regional or minority languages as an expression of cultural wealth;
> Respect for the geographical area of each regional or minority language;
> The need for resolute action to promote regional or minority languages;

Table 1.2 ECRML measures summarised by article

Article 8 – Education (Members must choose at least three articles)	Measures from pre-school to tertiary and adult / continuing education to include RMLs.
Article 9 – Judicial authorities (Members must choose at least one article)	Measures in criminal, civil and administrative proceedings to allow for the use of RMLs, including provisions for language services (translation and interpreting). Emphasis is placed on the legal validity of legal documents drafted in RMLs, as well as on the need to provide RML versions of the most relevant national statutory texts.
Article 10 – Administrative authorities and public services (Members must choose at least one article)	Comprehensive measures to actively include RMLs in public services; to allow RML speakers to submit documents and queries in RMLs and receive a reply in the same language; to appoint public service employees who speak RMLs in areas where the languages in question are in demand; to recruit and train public service employees with a view to including RMLs; to provide language services; to allow for the adoption of family names in RMLs.
Article 11 – Media (Members must choose at least one article)	Measures to "encourage and/or facilitate" the production of media, including radio, television and printed media, in RMLs, along with steps to offer financial assistance to productions and training of staff in RMLs. The freedom to receive and/or retransmit radio and TV broadcasts in RMLs across borders is also stipulated in one article, as well as the need to "guarantee[e] the freedom and pluralism of the media," ensuring that the interests of RML speakers are represented in the relevant bodies.

Table 1.2 (Continued)

Article 12 – Cultural activities and facilities (Members must choose at least three articles)	Comprehensive measures encompassing "libraries, video libraries, cultural centres, museums, archives, academies, theatres and cinemas, as well as literary work and film production, vernacular forms of cultural expression, festivals and the culture industries, including *inter alia* the use of new technologies" and the use of RMLs, including financial support, recruitment of staff, creation of bodies and provisions for "translation, dubbing, post-synchronisation and subtitling activities" to promote access.
Article 13 – Economic and social life (Members must choose at least one article)	Measures to ensure that prohibitive legislation in relation to the use of RMLs is eliminated from all economic and social spheres; that the use of RMLs is encouraged; that documents are made available in RMLs; that financial and banking translations are available in RMLs; that social care facilities offer treatment in RMLs.
Article 14 – Transfrontier exchanges	Measures to foster and facilitate cross border cooperation in "culture, education, information, vocational training and permanent education" for the benefit of RMLs speakers.

Source: ECRML (www.coe.int/en/web/european-charter-regional-or-minority-languages/text-of-the-charter)

The facilitation and/or encouragement of the use of regional or minority languages, in speech and writing, in public and private life;

The provision of appropriate forms and means for the teaching and study of regional or minority languages at all appropriate stages;

The promotion of relevant transnational exchanges;

The prohibition of all forms of unjustified distinction, exclusion, restriction or preference relating to the use of a

regional or minority language and intended to discourage or endanger its maintenance or development;
The promotion by states of mutual understanding between all the country's linguistic groups.

However, signing does convey the intention to ratify eventually, which in turn entails choosing at least 35 measures out of the 68 to be enacted through legislation. Measures cannot be chosen freely, as there are set number per area – as outlined in Table 1.2.

So far, 34 members of the CoE have signed the ECRML, out of which 25 have ratified it. As the reader will notice, the interview with Ó Riain took place before Portugal signed the Charter in September 2021. However, as the country has not yet ratified the Charter, the number of languages protected by it remains the same – 79. If it ever ratifies the Charter, Portugal is likely to add Mirandés, an Asur-Leonese language spoken in Terra de Miranda, in the northeast of Portugal, and recognised officially as the country's sole regional language (see Table 1.4).

The ECRML relies on a Committee of Experts (COMEX) comprised of one representative appointed by each participating state (i.e., signatories that ratified the ECRML) for a six-year mandate eligible for one re-appointment. The role of the experts is to monitor and report on RMLs in their respective country. At the time of writing, Bosnia and Herzegovina, Liechtenstein, Luxembourg and the United Kingdom have no experts allocated to them – at least not according to the ECRML website.[1]

The ECRML comprises a monitoring system whereby participating states must submit their first report on the implementation of the chosen articles within a year of ratification. Originally, states were also expected to submit subsequent reports every three years – a system heavily criticised for not having any follow-up arrangements in place and not imposing any penalties on states which did not comply with the selected ECRML articles and/or which did not submit the expected reports.

In light of these criticisms, in November 2018, decision CM(2018)165 was taken to strengthen the monitoring mechanism of the Charter. As of July 2019, participating states must submit periodical reports every *five* – rather than every *three* – years. However, the follow-up process has become more stringent.

Table 1.3 The ECRML by signature and ratification

State or International Organisation	Signature	Ratification
Armenia	11/05/2001	25/01/2002
Austria	05/11/1992	28/06/2001
Azerbaijan	21/12/2001	*
Bosnia and Herzegovina	07/09/2005	21/09/2010
Croatia	05/11/1997	05/11/1997
Cyprus	12/11/1992	26/08/2002
Czech Republic	09/11/2000	15/11/2006
Denmark	05/11/1992	08/09/2000
Finland	05/11/1992	09/11/1994
France	07/05/1999	*
Germany	05/11/1992	16/09/1998
Hungary	05/11/1992	26/04/1995
Iceland	07/05/1999	*
Italy	27/06/2000	*
Liechtenstein	05/11/1992	18/11/1997
Luxembourg	05/11/1992	22/06/2005
Malta	05/11/1992	*
Montenegro	22/03/2005	15/02/2006
Netherlands	05/11/1992	02/05/1996
North Macedonia	25/07/1996	*
Norway	05/11/1992	10/11/1993
Poland	12/05/2003	12/02/2009
Portugal	07/09/2021	*
Republic of Moldova	11/07/2002	*
Romania	17/07/1995	29/01/2008
Serbia	22/03/2005	15/02/2006
Slovak Republic	20/02/2001	05/09/2001
Slovenia	03/07/1997	04/10/2000
Spain	05/11/1992	09/04/2001
Sweden	09/02/2000	09/02/2000
Switzerland	08/10/1993	23/12/1997
Ukraine	02/05/1996	19/09/2005
United Kingdom	02/03/2000	27/03/2001
Russian Federation	10/05/2001	**

Albania, Andorra, Belgium, Bulgaria, Estonia, Georgia, Greece, Ireland, Latvia, Lithuania, Monaco, San Marino and Türkiye have not signed the ECRML.

Source: Chart of signatures and ratifications of Treaty 148 – Status as of 23/08/2022 (www.coe.int/en/web/conventions/full-list?module=signatures-by-treaty&treatynum=148)

* These countries have not (yet) ratified the ECRML.
** Russia's signature was suspended in March 2022.

Table 1.4 The 79 ECRML languages by country status as of 1 August 2022

Language	State
Albanian	Bosnia and Herzegovina, Montenegro, Romania, Serbia
Aragonese	Spain
Aranese	Spain
Armenian	Cyprus, Hungary, Poland, Romania
Assyrian	Armenia
Asturian	Spain
Basque	Spain
Belarusian	Poland, Ukraine
Bosnian	Montenegro, Serbia
Boyash	Hungary
Bulgarian	Hungary, Romania, Serbia, Slovakia, Ukraine
Bunjevac	Serbia
Catalan	Spain
Cornish	United Kingdom
Crimean Tatar	Ukraine
Croatian	Austria, Czech Republic, Hungary, Montenegro, Romania, Serbia, Slovakia, Slovenia
Cypriot Maronite Arabic	Cyprus
Czech	Austria, Bosnia and Herzegovina, Croatia, Poland, Romania, Serbia, Slovakia
Danish	Germany
Finnish	Sweden
Franco-Provençal	Switzerland
French	Switzerland
Frisian	Netherlands
Gagauz	Ukraine
Galician	Spain
German	Armenia, Bosnia and Herzegovina Croatia, Czech Republic, Denmark, Hungary, Poland, Romania, Serbia, Slovakia, Slovenia, Switzerland, Ukraine
Greek	Armenia, Hungary, Romania, Ukraine
Hungarian	Austria, Bosnia and Herzegovina, Croatia, Romania, Serbia, Slovakia, Slovenia, Ukraine
Inari Sámi	Finland
Irish	United Kingdom
Istro-Romanian	Croatia
Italian	Bosnia and Herzegovina, Croatia, Romania, Slovenia, Switzerland

Table 1.4 (Continued)

Language	State
Karaim	Poland, Ukraine
Karelian	Finland
Kashub	Poland
Krimchak	Ukraine
Kurdish	Armenia
Kven/Finnish	Norway
Ladino	Bosnia and Herzegovina
Lemko	Poland
Leonese	Spain
Limburgish	Netherlands
Lithuanian	Poland
Low German	Germany
Lower Saxon	Netherlands
Lower Sorbian	Germany
Lule Sámi	Norway, Sweden
Macedonian	Romania, Serbia
Manx Gaelic	United Kingdom
Meänkieli	Sweden
Moldovan	Ukraine
North Frisian	Germany
North Sámi	Finland, Norway, Sweden
Polish	Bosnia and Herzegovina, Czech Republic, Hungary, Romania, Slovakia, Ukraine
Romani (Romany, Romanes, Romani Chib, Roma language)	Austria, Bosnia and Herzegovina, Czech Republic, Finland, Germany, Hungary, Montenegro, Netherlands Norway, Poland, Romania, Serbia, Slovakia, Slovenia, Sweden, Ukraine
Romanian	Bosnia and Herzegovina, Croatia, Hungary, Serbia, Ukraine
Romansh	Switzerland
Russian	Armenia, Finland, Poland, Romania, Slovakia, Ukraine
Ruthenian	Bosnia and Herzegovina, Croatia, Hungary, Romania, Serbia, Slovakia, Ukraine
Sater Frisian	Germany
Scots	United Kingdom
Scottish-Gaelic	United Kingdom
Serbian	Croatia, Hungary, Romania, Slovakian, Slovenia
Skolt Sámi	Finland

(Continued)

Table 1.4 (Continued)

Language	State
Slovak	Austria, Bosnia and Herzegovina, Croatia, Czech Republic, Hungary, Poland, Romania, Serbia, Ukraine
Slovenian	Austria, Bosnia and Herzegovina, Croatia, Hungary
South Sámi	Norway, Sweden
Swedish	Finland
Tatar	Finland, Poland, Romania
Turkish	Bosnia and Herzegovina, Romania
Ukrainian	Armenia, Bosnia and Herzegovina, Croatia, Hungary, Poland, Romania, Serbia, Slovakia
Ulster Scots	United Kingdom
Upper Sorbian	Germany
Valencian	Spain
Vlach	Serbia
Welsh	United Kingdom
Yenish	Switzerland
Yezidi	Armenia
Yiddish	Bosnia and Herzegovina, Finland, Netherlands, Poland, Romania, Slovakia, Sweden, Ukraine

Source: www.coe.int/en/web/european-charter-regional-or-minority-languages/languages-covered

Following the submission of the periodical report by a given state, a COMEX delegation is sent to that state to conduct talks not only with governmental bodies but also with NGOs, relevant associations and RML speakers. The COMEX then issues an evaluation report containing recommendations and makes it available to the public via the ECRML website. Within two months of publication of the evaluation report, any party may submit comments to it and/or request a confidential dialogue with the committee. Any comments submitted are also made available online. The state in question must then issue a response regarding the implementation of those recommendations deemed "for immediate action" in the COMEX evaluation report. This response must be released within two-and-a-half years of the submission of the periodical report.

The European Charter for Regional or Minority Languages 11

A glimpse through recent periodical reports from participating states, COMEX evaluation reports and so-called infoRIAs (information documents on the implementation of the recommendations for immediate action) issued by states, reveals that the new system looks promising. Concrete and relevant recommendations for immediate action are issued by COMEX, such as the following:[2]

- Cornish in the UK: "Devolve responsibility and provide funding to the County of Cornwall and Cornwall Council for the promotion of Cornish" (infoRIA UK, 5/1/2021, p. 2);
- Romani in Slovenia: "Start teaching Romani as a subject at all appropriate levels and develop a scheme for the training of teachers able to teach Romani" (infoRIA Slovenia, 22/4/2021, p. 9);
- Swedish and Sámi languages in Finland: "Take further measures to ensure the accessibility of social and health care in Swedish and in the Sámi languages" (infoRIA Finland, 4/3/2020, p. 4).

Recommendations such as these effectuate – or at least attempt to effectuate – the articles in the Charter which, in turn, are vague and filled with such verbs as "facilitate" and "encourage" the use of RMLs in various contexts. States can still be dismissive in their infoRIAs in some regards, but they are forced to address each and every recommendation requiring immediate action.

At the time of writing, a few countries are behind with their periodical reports and/or with their infoRIAs, namely Bosnia and Herzegovina, Cyprus, Luxembourg, Montenegro, Poland and Ukraine. The Charter relies on an intricate system of hierarchical reminders, but there is little the CoE can do other than issuing warnings. Nor did the 2018 reform fully address the problem of non-compliance with the ECRML articles chosen by the state in question. There has been significant improvement in that COMEX now assesses the situation *in situ*, has conversations with interested parties and issues concrete recommendations to which states *must* react within a deadline. However, these reactions can be dismissive, as already noted, and it is very early to assess the states' rate of participation in and compliance with the new system. Out of the 23 reports expected by August 2022 since the implementation of the reform, only six countries are behind, so a 74 per cent rate of compliance is perhaps enough reason for cautious optimism.

The field of language policy and the politics of language is riddled with a "do as I say, not as I do" attitude, whereby a favourable discourse towards language diversity, along with favourable language policies and ideologies, fly in the face of actual language practices, which – particularly but not exclusively in Europe – boil down to monolingualism in English (see Leal 2021). In this context, it is good news that the text of the ECRML has two authentic versions, namely in English and French, as well as versions in its two additional working languages, namely German and Italian. The Charter is nonetheless also available in a whopping 52 languages – though it remains unclear in which circumstances the translations were produced and who footed the bill. Moreover, it would be desirable to have the Charter available in all 79 languages to which it applies, to ensure that the relevant communities are informed of their rights and can actively participate, for instance, in the monitoring system. The ECRML website is available in the four official and working languages English and French, and Italian and German, respectively, but certain tabs, such as the news, are only available in English. COMEX reports and recommendations are always issued in English and French – even when the state in question submitted their periodical report in English only, such as Montenegro, Poland and the UK in recent years. COMEX reports are sometimes also available in the official language(s) of the state in question, albeit not systematically.

Finally, let us bear in mind that the Council of Europe and the European Union are two separate entities. The latter does have a "Council of the European Union," which is often referred to as the "European Council" and, for obvious reasons, confused with the Council of Europe. The EU has, nevertheless, fully endorsed the ECRML and urged all EU member states to sign and ratify it through the Killilea Resolution of 1994. Out of the 27 EU member states, four have signed the ECRML but not (yet) ratified it, namely France, Italy, Malta and Portugal, whereas seven countries – Belgium, Bulgaria, Estonia, Greece, Ireland, Latvia and Lithuania – have never signed it. Roughly 40 per cent of EU member states are hence ECRML countries, which is not an excellent figure given the (theoretical) prominence of linguistic diversity in the EU.

Let us look behind the scenes of the ECRML in the interview that follows and come back to some of these introductory remarks and criticisms in the last section of this chapter.

Interview

1 *Between August 1988 and September 1990, you were involved in the negotiations behind the Council of Europe's European Charter for Regional or Minority Languages (ECRML) as the representative of the Irish Government. The ECRML has recently celebrated its 20th anniversary. Could you tell us more about the challenges involved in the process?*
A. In August 1988 I was appointed Irish government representative in the Council of Europe committee charged with drawing up a charter on regional and minority languages. It was an intergovernmental committee – basically, representatives of the 23 member states of the Council of Europe, which comprised, at the time, all of Western Europe. It was before the collapse of communism and the reunification of Europe, and included Finland and San Marino, which were the last two countries to join. We managed to have one observer included – an Irishman, Dónall Ó Riagáin, Secretary General of the European Bureau for Less-Used Languages. He was an expert in the area, but some countries resisted the idea, insisting that it should be strictly intergovernmental. However, we pointed out to them that the European Bureau of Less-Used Languages was financed by the Irish government, the government of Catalonia and a number of other governments, but also by the European Commission. A lot of the financing came from the Commission, so we said, "Well, this is financed by the European Commission, so it can be seen as including the European Commission's expert in the minority language area, as an observer with the right to attend and to speak, but not to vote." This was very important because Ó Riagáin made a major contribution as an expert in the area; he was a very experienced negotiator. Normally he didn't speak until the end, having heard the positions of all the different countries. And then he would come in with a compromise proposal taking something from the positions of all the different countries. More often than not, his proposal was accepted, so he probably had more influence upon the result than many countries – he had a huge positive influence in the area.

We actually never had votes – we had discussions and eventually arrived at a consensus decision. Sometimes it took days, it took a long, long discussion. The majority of the group were in favour of a legally binding convention, and not a recommendation. This was one of the only things we actually voted on right towards the end of the negotiations. A clear majority of the countries' representatives wanted a strong convention to do as much as possible for the rights of minority languages and their speakers. A small group of countries had a different point of view: France, Greece, Turkey – and the United Kingdom to an extent. The UK was not quite as radical as the other three, who were strongly committed to the idea of one country, one language. The French colleagues did not wish to be too closely associated with the policy of Turkey – they were very clearly uncomfortable. I decided, as I speak French fluently, that I would speak in French only. Even when I disagreed with the French official position, it had some influence to have the Irish delegation speaking in French only.

At least half of those present spoke in French. French and English were the two languages used in Council of Europe discussions, and all present understood both. We had a Norwegian chairman, who spoke very good French. He was from the west of Norway, Bergen, and he used Nynorsk. The discussion continued for well over two years, for some time after I left (I was posted to Australia at the end of 1990). By then we had taken the most important decision: that the text would have the character of a legally binding convention and not a recommendation.

France, Greece and Turkey were arguing against a legally binding convention, and the United Kingdom was represented by a Welsh speaker from the Welsh office, who realised that UK policy was quite lukewarm on a legally binding convention, and said that he would probably get an instruction to vote against if he were to seek instructions. To avoid such an outcome, he decided not to seek instructions, which meant that, when we voted between a legally binding convention or a recommendation which could be forgotten about, the UK colleague was able to say, "I have no instructions from London, so I have to abstain." A UK abstention was an important step on the way toward a convention.

Only one country voted against: Greece. Both France and Turkey said that, as they were in a very small minority, they would abstain. Greece voted against and, at this stage, had the power to prevent a convention, because the decision had to be unanimous. However, the Greek representative very generously said something along the lines of, "We are conscious that we have the power to block a convention, due to the unanimity rule; but as no other country wishes to block a convention, we will not use this power. We will vote against, as Greece's position is that we should not have this convention on minority languages. We believe that all citizens in Greece should speak Greek." The Turkish colleague agreed that all citizens of Turkey should speak Turkish – so on this issue they agreed. The Greek representative said, "We are voting for a recommendation and not for a convention. At the same time, if the vast majority supports a convention, then we agree that it can be a convention." Thus was born the European Charter for Regional or Minority Languages – it opened for signature on 5 November 1992. It had been a fascinating discussion.

At that time, François Mitterrand was president of France and, as a socialist, he had given speeches quite favourable to regional and minority languages. On one occasion, I remember that I photocopied a speech from President Mitterrand from *Le Monde* and handed it to the French, and their general line had been to weaken the text. On one occasion, there was a proposal that speakers of regional or minority languages who work as public servants and wished to work in an area where that language was spoken, should have their request favourably considered. For instance, a Basque speaker who wanted to work in the Basque-speaking part of France, or a Breton who wanted to work in Brittany. France opposed this, saying that to accept it would be discriminating against everybody else who doesn't speak a minority language. I replied publicly: "We need to ask ourselves a fundamental question here: are we working on a convention in *favour* of regional and minority languages, or are we working on a convention *against* regional and minority languages?" So it wasn't blocked and became a convention.

2 *The ECRML is undoubtedly the boldest and most successful attempt to protect and foster regional and minority languages in Europe. So far, 25 states have signed and ratified it, whereas another eight have signed but not ratified it. Thanks to it, 79 language communities enjoy certain protections and rights in these 25 countries. However, the ECRML has been criticised for not*

enabling a control system coupled with penalties in case signatories breach the articles ratified. It has also been condemned for giving signatories free rein to define the notion of "regional or minority language" and freely choose which ones to protect. Another aspect of the ECRML that has drawn a lot of criticism is its exclusion of migrant languages. How do you see these shortcomings against the backdrop of the 20th anniversary of the ECMRL and its many successes?

A. There were quite a number of criticisms of the Charter, as you mention, and all of them were extensively discussed at the time. The reason that the convention is as it is – with the weaknesses mentioned – is because, politically, it would not have been possible to go any further. We pushed it as far as we could. There were several countries opposed to a convention, and they allowed it to come about, despite their opposition in principle. There were many attempts to strengthen it. One colleague suggested that we extend its rights to migrants, and immediately the reply came, "In London alone we have speakers of over 350 immigrant languages. How can you possibly organise public services in a way to provide services in 350 languages? Pragmatically, you cannot do this." The suggestion ran into this wall right away.

The word "autochthonous" was used in the text to denote languages that have been spoken for a very long time in an area, e.g., Breton in Brittany and Basque in the Basque country. No date was set, no specific number of centuries, but the words "autochthonous language" were used to exclude the languages of recent immigrants from a practical point of view. The committee did not see how it could be possible to organise things practically if recognition were given to every language spoken by every recent immigrant. There was also an idea that immigrants often come from countries whose languages are spoken at home by large populations. In Turkey, there are over 80 million speakers of Turkish, so the language is not threatened. Similarly, Pakistani or Chinese immigrants all speak widespread languages, which are under no threat. We felt that our committee should concern itself with languages which were really under threat of disappearance, like Breton or Basque, which are community languages only in their original territories. If they disappeared, they would be gone forever. The committee felt that a distinction needed to be made between the languages of immigrants who are speaking a language under no threat of disappearance, and languages that could completely disappear if they are not protected. This concerns speakers of a majority language, which happens to spill over into another country, such as German speakers in Belgium, about 70,000, or the French speakers in the Valle d'Aosta in Italy. They share many problems with speakers of other less used languages, like Breton and Basque. Most Belgians do not have fluent German, so it is not possible to do everything in German in Belgium, even if one has the theoretical right to do so. The defence of German in Belgium is entirely laudable and important, but the future of the German language does not depend on it. On the other hand, if Breton disappears in Brittany, it would no longer exist as a community language. The same is true of Irish, Scottish Gaelic, Welsh, Galician and Catalan. The latter appears to be quite a strong language and not in danger of disappearing at present.

A further point under discussion was the degree of difference of a language from its neighbouring languages. Basque and the Celtic languages are very different from neighbouring languages. Breton is very different from French, whereas Catalan has many features in common with French and Spanish/Castilian. This was not a criterion, but it was discussed. Languages like Basque are *sui generis*, and the committee felt that there is therefore a special reason to protect them, as an important part of the linguistic heritage of humanity. In addition, Catalan was seen to be in a stronger position and was not threatened with disappearance in the sense that Irish or Scottish Gaelic could disappear entirely. So, all these factors were involved.

3 The eight States that have signed but not ratified the ECRML are Azerbaijan, France, Iceland, Italy, Malta, Moldova, North Macedonia and Russia. The States that have neither signed, nor ratified the ECRML include Albania, Andorra, Belgium, Bulgaria, Estonia, Georgia, Greece, Ireland, Latvia, Lithuania, Monaco, Portugal, San Marino and Turkey. The reasons behind these countries' reluctance to join the ECRML are too multifaceted to be discussed here at length, but would you like to comment on general trends and difficulties you identify in these States and possible solutions to promote the Charter there?
A. They all have different reasons. Initially Greece and Turkey were very much against it. They felt threatened by minorities – we

spoke a lot in private to the Greek colleagues, who explained their reasoning to us. They said that there were Turkish-speaking minorities along the border with Turkey, and they felt that if Greece gave any recognition to these linguistic minorities, it could encourage them to agitate for union with Turkey, and Greece could lose some territory. In addition to this problem was the perception that Greek was a small language with a very long history. They strongly believed that everybody living in Greece should speak Greek, and that those who did not speak Greek should learn it. The delegates felt that public services in Greece should be offered in Greek only, and everybody should be able to avail of them in Greek. They had quite a strong attitude, possibly due to their minority position historically in the Ottoman Empire. They feared that recognising minority languages in Greece could ultimately threaten territorial unity. For example, Ó Riagáin told me that a colleague of his was travelling in Greece trying to record speakers of minority languages in different villages, and he believed he was being followed by the police, who saw his activity as possibly hostile to the Greek state. France also believed that all French citizens should speak French.

The Turkish colleagues tended to see official recognition of Kurdish as encouraging demands to recognise an independent Kurdistan, which would include much of southeast Turkey. They therefore opposed the granting of any recognition to Kurdish as a language. It was strange to have Turkey and Greece, who disagreed politically on many issues at that time, supporting each other regarding minority languages. Sometimes I would refer to "*la position franco-turque,*" and the French colleagues would try to distance themselves in some way from the Turkish view. However, in reality, France, Turkey and Greece were all aiming to weaken the Charter.

The UK may have favoured weakening the Charter, but it was represented by a Welsh speaker from the Welsh Office whose contribution was entirely in favour of strengthening it. He made a vital contribution to gaining an abstention from the UK, rather than a negative vote. If the UK had voted against, together with Greece, that would probably have encouraged France and Turkey to vote against. The text would then have become a recommendation, not a legally binding convention. There are hundreds of these recommendations, which have no legal force, and tend to be ignored and forgotten. This Welsh colleague therefore played a crucial role. His colleagues in London may not have been impressed, but the supporters of minority languages in all parts of Europe can thank him for his fine work.

My own country, Ireland, has neither signed nor ratified the Charter. A number of us, including Ó Riagáin, tried to persuade Ireland to sign and ratify, even if just to show political support, by declaring something like "Ireland has no minority or regional language, but signing is a mark of support for linguistic diversity." However, it was considered that this would not be compatible with the constitutional position of the Irish language as the only national language and first official language of Ireland. The Irish version of the Constitution says in Article 8: "*Ós í an Ghaeilge an teanga náisiúnta is í an phríomhtheanga oifigiúil í,*" or "As Irish is the national language, it is the principal official language." The English version says Irish is the *first* official language, while the Irish version says it is the *principal* official language. English is recognised in the English version as the *second* official language; in Irish, English is called "*teanga oifigiúil eile,*" which means "*another* official language." In addition, one of the subsections of article 25 clearly states that, in case of differences between the English and Irish versions of this constitution, "the text in the national language shall prevail."

Irish has a stronger position in the constitution than English, even though it is spoken by far less than 50 per cent of the people in Ireland, probably by about 2 per cent as an everyday language. It is not the Constitution which made Irish the national language: the Constitution merely recognised that Irish is, in fact, the ancestral and national language of Ireland. For instance, the majority of place names and surnames throughout the island of Ireland make sense only in Irish, not in English. The same is true for most of Scotland as well. Right up to the English border, you get Gaelic place names. Edinburgh's old name was *Dùn Èideann*, "the fortress of *Èideann*," and *dùn* is a Gaelic word, which is very common in place names in both Ireland and Scotland. I once flew to Edinburgh and on the bus to the city centre I saw five place names of Gaelic origin. Some claim Gaelic was never spoken in the Lothians. If that were true, the question arises as to why the region has so many place names of Gaelic origin.

The same applies to surnames. One of the strongest opponents of official status for Irish in Northern Ireland, Gregory Campbell, has a purely Gaelic surname: "*cam beul*" means "crooked mouth."

The former British Prime Minister, David Cameron, *"cam shrón"* means "crooked nose" in Gaelic. Both those surnames are of Gaelic origin, so denying the status of Irish or Scottish Gaelic is, in a sense, denying their own family origins. There is a common Gaelic past in the two countries. Up to 1800 the same Gaelic Bible was in use in Ireland and Scotland. It was the Irish version, but the first book published in Irish was printed in Scotland in 1567 and was in use in the two countries. It was Bishop John Carswell's *Foirm na n-Urrnuidheadh*, a translation of John Knox's liturgy, in Classical Common Gaelic. A specifically Scottish Gaelic version of the bible was produced around 1800, a very poetic translation. With such a history it would have been difficult for any Irish government to classify Irish as a "minority or regional" language in Ireland.

Other countries have their own or several particular reasons for not signing and/or ratifying. It is a political decision. The Baltic states, possibly due to reluctance to recognise the Russian and Polish language minorities. San Marino doesn't have minority languages. Turkey again has this reluctance to give recognition to Kurdish, for political reasons.

[Italy is interesting because it has many languages spoken in its territory. It has signed but not ratified.]

Yes, that is interesting, signing normally means an intention to ratify, eventually. I read that, until World War II, the majority of Italians didn't speak Italian but their own dialect. Only since World War II has the beautiful Italian language become the everyday language and the most used language in Italy, a unifying factor. I think that the reason for reluctance to ratify may be connected to concerns regarding the unity of the country. That is the case in France, for instance. Those who oppose ratifying the Charter argue that it could eventually impact on territorial unity.

There is a certain idea that territorial unity depends on monolingualism, which is firmly entrenched in officialdom in many countries. The idea is particularly strong in France. I know some Esperanto speakers in France who are generally left wing and liberal, but they would not support ratifying the Charter, because they would see it as a danger to French unity. The fact that the Charter has not been ratified by these countries – going back to the earlier discussion – shows that this Charter really was the maximum achievable at that time. Having gone any further in strengthening provisions for regional and minority languages would probably have meant four countries voting against, so it would never have become a legally binding convention, and would have remained a recommendation, with little to no effect. The intergovernmental committee was aware that one step further was too far and that we risked losing everything. The committee did as much in favour of minority languages as was possible at that time, in my view.

[I find it interesting that language questions are usually dismissed or often dismissed as irrelevant, but as soon as you talk about, for example, granting rights to minorities, it becomes something dangerous. It's dangerous to give rights to minorities, minorities might threaten unity. It's paradoxical.]

Absolutely. There is an idea, shared by many, particularly those who do not think much about languages, that language is just a means of communication, just a code, and that different languages are just different ways of saying the same thing. But that is a very limited understanding of human language, which overlooks much of the research. Every language expresses a particular culture and history, a particular *Weltanschauung*, and there are things which can be said in each language, like *wunschlos glücklich* in German, which are difficult to translate. There are specific concepts in every language ... a *gentleman* in English, for instance, or the Irish word *dúchas*, which means that which you have inherited, something that comes naturally to you, that you never needed to learn. There is no adequate English word for it.

[And even if you tried to explain, right, I mean such a foreign concept that you can't quite grasp...]

...exactly.

[Well, I think we can probably strike this part of the question which asks whether you identify any general trends that might push these countries to sign or to ratify the ECRML. I think the context of each country is too individual, and if I understand you correctly, most cases probably have more to do with this mentality of protection of unity, so something would have to change in that regard.]

I think so, exactly. It's a kind of nationalistic trait, really, the unity of the nation. It does not apply to Europe so far, however, as many people see Europe as something which doles out money or which may have some relevance to the climate area, as a large

collection of countries, but there isn't this emotional link to Europe, for most people.
[It's growing, but it's still incipient.]

Commentary

Ó Riain argues repeatedly that the ECRML is a delicate compromise, precariously achieved in negotiations which could easily have turned sour had there been a push for migrant languages, for instance, or a more stringent monitoring system. 20 years after entering into force, the achievements of the ECMRL remain modest. As noted above, about 40 per cent of EU member states have ratified it, while 54 per cent of the CoE have done so. The average interval between signature and ratification has been 4.8 years so far, with Croatia and Sweden signing and ratifying simultaneously and Luxemburg and Romania taking 13 years to ratify. Most signatures were collected in the 1990s and early 2000s, with the sole exception of Portugal in 2021. Among the signatories which have not yet ratified, an average of 23.5 years has elapsed between the signature and the time of writing, with Portugal's signature only one and Malta's over 30 years ago.

France is a case in point here as it epitomises a lot of the concerns shared by nations which either have not signed the ECRML or have not ratified it. As noted by Ó Riain and outlined, for example, by Máiréad Nic Craith, first and foremost are fears over the "principles of unity" and the "indivisibility" of the nation (Nic Craith 2006, 161). These fears dovetail with concerns over the politicisation of language and the potential use of the ECRML as a political tool in separatist and nationalist movements. Nils Ringe, for example, welcomes the mismatch between the EU's pledge to protect and foster multilingualism and the English-language monolingualism of its institutions, bodies and agencies as it prevents what he sees as the politicisation of language (Ringe 2022). Is the choice to use, protect or not protect a certain language not already a political decision, with clear political consequences (see Leal forthcoming)? And is the unity of the nation threatened more by the recognition of minorities or the *lack* thereof? The world is not short of examples of revolutions kick-started precisely by the lack of recognition of certain languages and their speakers. Think of the riots in Soweto which culminated in the end of Apartheid following the introduction of Afrikaans into the curriculum, or the increasingly monolingual policies introduced by the Milošević government in former Yugoslavia ahead of the civil war (see Leal 2021, 71 – see also Kraus 2018, 90–91 for further examples). Moreover, the association between language minorities and nationalist / populist movements constitutes a common misconception, as argued convincingly, for instance, by Peter A. Kraus in his recent works (see, e.g., Kraus 2021).

In addition to concerns over the unity of the nation, Ó Riain mentions the argument that it is impossible to cater to hundreds of languages in a city like London in the debate surrounding the recognition of migrant languages and/or additional RMLs. But this would be tantamount to saying that one cannot adapt, say, a public building to *all* possible disabilities, so one should not cater to *any* disabilities whatsoever; one cannot have mainstream, fully plastic-free supermarkets, so there should be *no* efforts whatsoever to reduce plastic use; restaurants cannot avoid all possible allergens, so they should not have *any* alternatives whatsoever. Having information in *one* additional language is better than none, and it entails no obligation to issue information in every language spoken by every individual in a given territory.

The question of migrant languages also unveils the blind spots of the "rhetoric of indigeneity" (Nic Craith 2006, 172). Though the ECRML explicitly excludes "the languages of migrants" (see Article 1), its definition of RML is comprehensive enough to include non-indigenous – or to use an even more controversial term, allochthonous (more in Chapter 4) – languages. Witness, for example, the report drafted by Bernard Cerquiglini, former director of the *Institut National de la Langue Française* and former vice-president of the *Conseil Supérieur de la Langue Française* (currently rector of the *Agence universitaire de la Francophonie*), ahead of France's signature of the Charter in 1998. He listed 75 languages, spoken in French territory by substantial numbers of people, which fall within the definition of RML put forth in the Charter, including colloquial Arabic and Berber. Ironically, the report is partially blamed for the fact that France never ratified the ECRML (see Nic Craith 2006, 161).

Arabic is an interesting example of a widespread language in Europe, spoken between the eighth and the sixteenth century in the Iberian Peninsula and leaving a permanent imprint, for example, on Portuguese and Spanish. It is also the language spoken by millions of European citizens whose families originate from former colonies, particularly in the Maghreb region, as well as from so-called "guest workers," who migrated to Europe in the wake of the Second World War, and by very recent migrants, for example, from Syria. As noted by Ó Riain, those who argue against a need to protect Arabic within frameworks such as the ECRML claim that Arabic is one of the most widely spoken languages in the world and, thus, does not need protection. However, this argument focusses on the *language* rather than on the *individual*. Growing up speaking Arabic at home, say, in France, and not being able to use it beyond the home has clear consequences for the speakers; it has little to do with the representativity of Arabic across the globe.

Moreover – and perhaps more importantly – this notion of language as a monolithic unit – "the" Arabic language – is at odds with current developments in linguistics. Languages are plural and diverse within themselves in their dialects, sociolects, registers, etc. (see Nic Craith 2006, 160; Pennycook 2006; Johnson 2013). This, in turn, means that the Arabic language spoken, say, in Germany (itself a collection of different threads with the most varied origins) is an integral and unique part of "the" Arabic language, the loss of which also entails a loss of diversity in the world's linguistic landscape despite the continued presence of other threads of Arabic in other parts of the planet.

The issue of migrant languages, particularly in the EU, has become increasingly controversial and will re-emerge in Chapter 4. As Joshua A. Fishman remarked in 2006, the EU "has [not] made any effort whatsoever to extend any rights or courtesies to [its] manifold immigrant languages" (Fishman 2006, 314). Will Kymlicka's opposition between – and neoliberal rationale behind – "multination states" (i.e., countries with indigenous national minorities) and "polyethnic states" (i.e., nations with ethnic minorities resulting from immigration) holds sway in Europe and beyond. In Kymlicka's view, polyethnic states need not protect or foster migrant languages; instead, they must allow their use at home, leaving it up to individuals to speak them or not, while ensuring integration through the compulsory teaching of the national language(s) (see Kymlicka 1995, especially his Chapter 2; see also May 2006; Schmidt 2006; Skutnabb-Kangas 2006; Wee 2011, especially his Chapter 2; Ives 2015).

These views dovetail with the notions of "language-as-problem" and "language-as-right" as put forth by Richard Ruiz (2016). In his framework of language orientations, a "language-as-problem" orientation is grounded in the ideal of monolingualism in the official language, whereby the only acceptable form of "multilingualism" is bilingualism in the official language plus English (or another dominant language), as endorsed and promulgated by education systems. In the "language-as-problem" paradigm, home language use that differs from the official language(s) is perceived as a hurdle in the acquisition of the official language(s), as both linguistic and cultural assimilation is the ultimate goal. A "language-as-right" orientation is undergirded by the universal linguistic human rights movement, whereby speaking languages different from the official language(s) is perceived as a basic right, at least in the home. A combination of these two orientations lies beneath Kymlicka's views on "polyethnic states" and is widespread among decision-makers, for instance, in the EU (see Leal 2021).

These language-as-problem and as-right orientations miss the boat completely when it comes to the necessary "incentives and opportunities" (Hornberger 2006) to speak a language. Bernard Spolsky (based on David Crystal's work), for instance, argues that other factors lying beyond the remit of language policy are more relevant to the maintenance of minority languages, namely (1) "increased prestige;" (2) "increased legitimate power" and (3) "increase in wealth" in the "dominant community for speakers of the language;" (4) "a strong presence in the educational system;" (5) "a writing system;" and (6) "access to electronic technology" (Spolsky 2004, 215–216). On Spolsky's account, apart from factor 5, which falls within the realm of language policy, the other factors are social, economic, political and technological.

While it remains indisputable that language policy alone does not necessarily lead to transformed language practices and ideologies, it seems unrealistic to expect linguistic minorities, which are often in a subordinate position in their respective communities, to take full responsibility for the maintenance of linguistic diversity, without state provisions and without proper, state-sanctioned "incentives and opportunities" to use their languages (Hornberger 2006, 32 – see Leal 2021, 64–72). Particularly regarding migrant subordinate groups (Paulston & Heidemann 2006, 296), the full loss of their mother tongue usually occurs by the third generation, as Spolsky himself reports (2004, 44).

As Kraus puts it, languages can be assessed in terms of the ties and gates that they entail. Based on Karl Dahrendorf's theory of options and ligatures (1979), Kraus argues that there is a relational function between our ties (ligatures or bonds) to our language(s) and the gates that these languages open – or, in other words, the options that they offer (Kraus 2018, 95). Take migrant languages as an example: while there may be, initially, strong emotional ties to these languages due to the role they play in their speakers' lifeworld, second and, at the latest, third-generation speakers lose these ligatures as these languages do not open any gates to them in their new home. In other words, without incentives and opportunities to use a language, ligatures are lost and new ones are formed to official language(s) plus English (see Leal 2021, 141–144). We will revisit the theory of options and ligatures in Chapter 5. But to come back to Spolsky's six factors listed earlier, it is unimaginable that subordinate migrant groups should be in a position to increase their prestige, legitimate power and wealth, while forging a strong presence for their language in education systems *and* guaranteeing access to electronic technology in that language.

This is where Ruiz's third language orientation comes into play, namely a "language-as-resource" orientation. Through this orientation, the monolingual ideal (i.e., the state language plus English model) is replaced through the multilingual ideal. The multilingualism present in society – be it through the existence of indigenous ethnic minorities or the influx of migrant communities – is tapped into as an asset, resulting in multilingual education for minority and majority language speakers alike and incentives and opportunities to use different languages in public life (Ruiz 2016, 14 – see also Johnson 2013, 36).

Most of the ECRML measures are clear attempts to produce widespread, relevant and state-subsidised incentives and opportunities for RMLs to be used across all realms of public life; they are a clear attempt to move away from the "language-as-problem" orientation, while consolidating the "language-as-right" orientation to ensure at the very least that RML speakers learn to read and write in their language(s) and can go on to study them at university. Yet the ECRML measures go beyond that by trying to engender a "language-as-resource" orientation as well, through a heightened and active presence of RMLs in society. But even if the ECRML were to explicitly include migrant languages, if states were willing to sign, ratify and expand the range of languages to which the ECRML applies in their territory, this would not guarantee equity among language communities. Take Roma communities as an example: a 2020 EU report reveals gross and widespread discrimination taking place in states that have ratified the ECRML and chosen to protect and foster Roma languages (European Commission 2020). Ironically, *there is not a single mention of language* in the report. This underlines the conundrum outlined earlier in relation to Spolsky's arguments that the jurisdiction of language policy is limited, and social, political, economic and technological changes are required to protect and promote languages. It is indisputable that discrimination against Roma communities is not a purely linguistic phenomenon; yet the language question is *inseparable* from all other relevant realms of society. The Roma example reveals that initiatives such as the ECRML – though instrumental at the very least so that a dialogue about linguistic minorities is initiated and maintained (see Nic Craith 2006; Paulston & Heidemann 2006, 298; de Witte 2008) – need to be expanded and made more stringent and fluid to keep up with the changing linguistic landscape of societies today.

As Ó Riain argues indirectly, the move from a "language-as-problem" and "as-right" to a "language-as-resource" orientation requires a stronger sense of identification with the EU and not just with the member states; put differently, it requires a move from a national to a more transnational orientation (see Leal 2021, 127–128). Since 1982, the EU has been monitoring the levels of citizen identification in its Standard Eurobarometer surveys – albeit through slightly different questions, thus precluding the identification of a single, clear trend. Presumably this did not feature in previous Eurobarometer surveys, which began in 1974, because the EU started turning itself to issues of identification from the 1980s, with the Tindemans Report in 1976, the Adonnino Committee in 1984, the adoption of the EU anthem and flag in 1985 and the Treaty of Maastricht in 1993.

At any rate, in 1982, 16 per cent of Eurobarometer participants "often thought of themselves as citizens of Europe" (as opposed to "sometimes," 37 per cent, and "never," 43 per cent) (European Commission 1982, 41–42). In 1992, 14 per cent answered "often," 32 per cent "sometimes" and 51 per cent "never" (European Commission 1992, 50). By 2006, 17 per cent "often" thought of themselves as European, 38 per cent "sometimes" and 42 per cent "never" (European Commission 2006, 112). Today, 56 per cent identify with the EU, as opposed to 14 per cent who do not identify with it – 28 per cent are "noncommittal" (European Commission 2021, 74). More research is required to ascertain to what extent these fluctuations are representative of an identification trend particular to the EU. Indeed, studies suggest that the levels of identification of citizens with their respective continents has increased in comparable levels, for instance, in Africa and South America (see, e.g., Roose 2013). We will come back to the thorny issue of a "European identity" in what follows.

Notes

1 See www.coe.int/en/web/european-charter-regional-or-minority-languages/members-of-the-committee-of-experts (last accessed in November 2022).
2 All periodical reports, evaluation reports and infoRIAs are available here: www.coe.int/en/web/european-charter-regional-or-minority-languages/reports-and-recommendations#{%2228993157%22:[24] (last accessed in November 2022).

References

Dahrendorf, Ralf. 1979. *Life chances: Approaches to social and political theory*. Chicago: The University of Chicago Press.
de Witte, Bruno. 2008. "The protection of linguistic diversity through provisions of the EU Charter other than Article 22." In *Respecting linguistic diversity in the European Union*, edited by Xabier Arzoz, 175–190. Amsterdam & Philadelphia: Benjamins.
European Commission. 1982. "Euro-barometre N. 17 June 1982." https://europa.eu/eurobarometer/surveys/detail/1443
European Commission. 1992. "Eurobarometer N. 37: Public Opinion in the European Community." https://europa.eu/eurobarometer/surveys/detail/1423
European Commission. 2006. "Eurobarometer 66: Public Opinion in the European Union." https://europa.eu/eurobarometer/surveys/detail/584

European Commission. 2020. "EU Roma strategic framework for equality, inclusion and participation for 2020 – 2030." https://ec.europa.eu/info/sites/info/files/union_of_equality_eu_roma_strategic_framework_for_equality_inclusion_and_participation_en.pdf.
European Commission. 2021. "Special Eurobarometer 508: Values and Identities of EU citizens." https://europa.eu/eurobarometer/surveys/detail/2230
Fishman, Joshua A. 2006. "Language policy and language shift." In *An introduction to language policy: Theory and method*, edited by Thomas Ricento, 311–328. Malden: Blackwell Publishing.
Hornberger, Nancy H. 2006. "Frameworks and models in language policy and planning." In *An introduction to language policy: Theory and method*, edited by Thomas Ricento, 24–41. Malden: Blackwell Publishing.
Ives, Peter. 2015. "Global English and the limits of liberalism: Confronting global capitalism and challenges to the nation-state." In *Language policy and political economy: English in a global context*, 48–71. Oxford: Oxford University Press.
Johnson, David Cassels. 2013. *Language policy*. London: Palgrave Macmillan.
Kraus, Peter A. 2018. "From glossophagic hegemony to multilingual pluralism?: Re-assessing the politics of linguistic identity in Europe." In *The politics of multilingualism: Europeanisation, globalisation and linguistic governance*, edited by François Grin and Peter A. Kraus, 89–109. Amsterdam & Philadelphia: John Benjamins.
Kraus, Peter. 2021. "Popular republicanism versus populism: Articulating the people." *Social Sciences* 10 (10).
Kymlicka, Will. 1995. *Multicultural citizenship: A liberal theory of minority rights*. Oxford: Oxford University Press.
Leal, Alice. 2021. *English and translation in the European Union: Unity and multiplicity in the wake of Brexit*. Abingdon & New York: Routledge.
Leal, Alice. forthcoming. "Nils Ringe. (2022) The language(s) of politics: Multilingual policymaking in the European Union, Michigan: University of Michigan Press. 280 pp." *Language problems and language planning*.
May, Stephen. 2006. "Language policy and minority rights." In *An introduction to language policy: Theory and method*, edited by Thomas Ricento, 255–272. Malden: Blackwell Publishing.
Nic Craith, Máiréad. 2006. *Europe and the politics of language: Citizens, migrants and outsiders*. New York: Palgrave Macmillan.
Paulston, Christina B., and Kai Heidemann. 2006. "Language policies and the education of linguistic minorities." In *An introduction to*

language policy: Theory and method, edited by Thomas Ricento, 292–310. Malden: Blackwell Publishing.

Pennycook, Alastair. 2006. "Postmodernism in language policy." In *An introduction to language policy: Theory and method*, edited by Thomas Ricento, 60–76. Malden: Blackwell Publishing.

Ringe, Nils. 2022. *The Language(s) of politics: Multilingual policy-making in the European Union*. Michigan: The University of Michigan Press.

Roose, Jochen. 2013. "How European is European identification? Comparing continental identification in Europe and beyond." *Journal of Common Market Studies* 51 (3): 281–297.

Ruiz, Richard. 2016. "Orientations in language planning." In *Honoring Richard Ruiz and his work on language planning and bilingual education*, edited by Nancy H. Hornberger, 13–32. Bristol: Multilingual Matters.

Schmidt, Ronald. 2006. "Political theory and language policy." In *An introduction to language policy: Theory and method*, edited by Thomas Ricento, 95–110. Malden: Blackwell Publishing.

Skutnabb-Kangas, Tove. 2006. "Language policy and linguistic human rights." In *An introduction to language policy: Theory and method*, edited by Thomas Ricento, 273–291. Malden: Blackwell Publishing.

Spolsky, B. 2004. *Language policy*. Cambridge: Cambridge University Press.

Wee, Lionel. 2011. *Language without rights*. Oxford: Oxford University Press.

2 The status of multilingualism in the European Commission

Introductory remarks

Multilingualism is enshrined in the European Union's (EU) treaties and in its motto, "united in diversity." In the present chapter, the interview with Seán Ó Riain traces the development of the multilingualism portfolio in the European Commission, while offering an overview and discussion of the political motivations behind its upgrading and subsequent downgrading, an appraisal of its current place in the Commission, as well as a description of attempts to engender more robust language policies (including a role for a neutral language).

Though present from day one, the question of multilingualism was not formally incorporated into the institutional framework of the EU (and its forerunner institutions) until the first Barroso Commission in 2004. As Abram De Swaan reported in 1993, "[t]here was much talk of milk pools and butter mountains, of a unitary currency, of liberalizing movements of EC citizens and restricting access for outsiders, but the language in which these issues were dealt with remained itself a non-issue" (1993, 244). Multilingualism only became a portfolio or, in fact, a part of the portfolio for Education, Training, Culture and Multilingualism, managed by Commissioner Ján Figeľ, in 2004. It relied on its own unit within the Directorate-General for Education and Culture. As Table 2.1 illustrates, multilingualism was briefly upgraded to an exclusive portfolio between 2007 and 2009, then downgraded to part of a portfolio between 2010 and 2014. In 2014, under Jean-Claude Junker, multilingualism was further downgraded as it disappeared from the title of the education portfolio. Consequently,

DOI: 10.4324/9781003342069-2

Table 2.1 Multilingualism in the European Commission

2004–2007 José Manuel Barroso	Education, Training, Culture and Multilingualism	Ján Figeľ (Slovakia)
2007–2009 José Manuel Barroso	Multilingualism portfolio	Leonard Orban (Romania)
2010–2014 José Manuel Barroso	Education, Culture, Multilingualism and Youth	Androulla Vassiliou (Cyprus)
2014–2019 Jean-Claude Junker	Education, Culture, Youth and Sport	Tibor Navracsics (Hungary)
2019–2024 Ursula Von der Leyen	Budget and Administration	Johannes Hahn (Austria)

the multilingualism unit of DG Culture and Education was also discontinued.

At the time of writing, under Ursula Von der Leyen, multilingualism has been moved from the realm of education to the sphere of administration. This must be understood in parallel with two further changes, namely the decision to move the Commission's Directorate-General for Translation (DGT), the EU's chief language service provider, under administration as well, and the decision to bestow upon DGT "policy-making" powers as "guarantor of multilingualism" in the EU (European Commission 2010, 57).

In the early days of the EU's forerunner institutions, i.e., between the 1950s and the mid-1980s, language services had traditionally been a part of the Directorate-General for Administration. It was during the Delors presidency that the then so-called "language services" were granted the status of Directorate-General in response to a strike by translators in the wake of an announcement that they would be moved to a new building far away from the Commission's headquarters (see European Commission 2010). The recent restructuring can thus be seen as a return of sorts to this previous arrangement, whereby language services are placed under what is now a commissioner's portfolio for administration – however, as a directorate-general with a remit in policy-making in the realm of multilingualism.

The quick upgrading of multilingualism in the Commission between 2007 and 2009 deserves a moment of our attention – and Ó Riain goes into it in this chapter's interview. At the time, the move conveyed a heightened – albeit short-lived, as it turned out – importance of linguistic diversity in the bloc's political set-up. Though framed by Barroso precisely along these lines, the upgrade was perceived by more cynical interpreters as a mere attempt to produce new portfolios swiftly for the then newly acceded members, Romania and Bulgaria (see Buck 2006; Leal 2021, 91, 186). Judging by the subsequent downgrading of the portfolio, one can speculate that this cynical interpretation was correct. We will come back to this question in the Commentary below.

The reader will notice that Ó Riain mentions a platform for multilingualism in what follows. He is referring to the ECSPM: the European Civil Society Platform for Multilingualism. It was originally put together by the Commission in October 2009 as the Civil Society Platform on Multilingualism, comprised of 29 non-governmental European organisations in the realm of language and multilingualism. Its original mandate was to produce a report in 2011, to which Ó Riain refers in his interview. The platform was relaunched in 2012, then again in 2013, before finally having its funding (which covered only travel expenses to meetings in Brussels) being withdrawn by the Commission in 2015. In 2016, the group was reshaped as the European Civil Society for Multilingualism, an NGO with a clearer emphasis on the "civil" society, completely independent from EU institutions. At the time of writing, there are 26 members, from research groups and platforms within universities across Europe to NGOs and associations in the area of language, culture and education. It must be noted, however, that the European Esperanto Union has recently decided to leave the ECS(P)M because of what they perceive as the Anglophone monolingualism of the society (private communications with Ó Riain).

The ECSPM 2011 report mentions the project "Springboard to languages," to which Ó Riain refers as well. Originally run by the University of Manchester, the project involved four primary schools (about 250 pupils) and aimed to raise their language awareness and prepare them for future language learning by teaching them basic Esperanto. The idea was to give them a taste of rapid language-learning success through Esperanto, a regular language through-and-through, before exposing them to other languages (see more in the interview). "Springboard to languages" gave rise to another project, also noted by Ó Riain in what follows, namely the "Multilingualism accelerator/MLA." Co-funded by

Erasmus+, the MLA is a curriculum to teach primary-school pupils basic Esperanto with the same aims as "Springboard to languages." We will come back to the acrimonious debate around a role for a planned language in the EU in the Commentary below.

Another topic discussed by Ó Riain in the context of civic participation in the EU is the ECI, or European Citizens' Initiative. The ECI is a platform in which citizens can ask the European Commission to bring forward legislative proposals, provided that the initiative falls within the EU's jurisdiction and successfully gathers at least 1 million supporters across a minimum of one quarter of the member states. To be more precise, "in at least one quarter of the Member States, the number of signatories [must be] at least equal to the minimum number set out in Annex I, corresponding to the number of the Members of the European Parliament elected in each Member State, multiplied by the total number of Members of the European Parliament, at the time of registration of the initiative" – see Regulation (EU) 2019/788. One of the most renowned ECIs so far, "Ban glyphosate and protect people and the environment from toxic pesticides," has been lauded for sparking an EU-wide debate on the controversial pesticide.

An example of an ECI that is directly relevant to us here is entitled "Minority SafePack," whose main objective is to "improve the protection of persons belonging to national and linguistic minorities and strengthen cultural and linguistic diversity in the Union" through the adoption of 11 legal acts.[1] Proposed in 2013, this ECI was initially rejected by the European Commission because it "manifestly fell outside the powers" of the EU. After all, language policy does not fall within EU jurisdiction and remains a sole prerogative of the member states.

The authors of the ECI appealed this decision and, on 3 February 2017, the Court of Justice of the EU agreed to publish the initiative, with the caveat that two out of the 11 legal acts proposed "manifestly fall outside the framework of the Commission's power to propose legislation." The ECI went on to gather 1,128,385 signatures across all the then 28 member states; it was officially submitted in January 2020 and had its public hearing in the European Parliament in October 2020. The feedback received was overwhelmingly positive, with a majority of MEPs present urging the Commission to adopt legal acts particularly to protect diversity within (and not just among) member states.

In December 2020, a whopping majority (524 out of 694 votes) in the European Parliament voted for a resolution supporting the intended outcomes of the ECI and once again urging the Commission to adopt legal acts. Resolutions, albeit not legally binding beyond the Parliament, can function as a call for action to compel the Commission to adopt binding legislation. This particular resolution, P9 TA(2020)0370, highlights the role of linguistic diversity as a "founding value" of the EU and embeds it in the bloc's legislative framework. More importantly, it underlines the need for the Commission to take this ECI seriously as a mechanism to increase civic participation in the EU.

Despite this, the Commission decided not to propose any legal acts in communication C(2021) 171 of January 2021, alleging that "no additional legal act is necessary" because of the "existing instruments and on-going initiatives" which, in the Commission's view, address all areas in which the ECI proposed legislative acts. In March 2021, members of the ECI filed a request for the annulment of the European Commission's decision in the General Court of the European Union. The process is still ongoing.

The fate of this particular ECI illustrates Ó Riain's views in his interview below regarding a lack of will by the Commission to allow for more active civic participation in the bloc's decision-making process. Moreover, it encapsulates the lack of awareness on the part of decision-makers as regards the implications of language questions, which Ó Riain also notes in what follows. We will return to some of these questions in the Commentary below.

Interview

4 *Addressing the European Union (EU) specifically, the multilingualism portfolio went from having its own Commissioner for a couple of years in the late 2000s under Barroso's Commission, to being incorporated into other portfolios and eventually being eliminated altogether under Juncker. Currently, multilingualism is under the auspices of the Directorate-General for Translation (DGT) of the European Commission – yet there is no specific unit dedicated to it. How do you see the development of the multilingualism portfolio in the bloc and what do you envision for the future?*
A. The development you outline is sad but true. It clearly shows a systemic failure in European integration. There is a lack of vision

among our political leaders. Most of them appear too immersed in day-to-day problems to be able to find time to study the scholarly literature on language policy. Thus, they either cannot see the need for action in this crucially important area, or they do not have the courage to take the necessary action. In 2007, I started working in the Commission, and we had for the first time ever a commissioner for multilingualism – Leonard Orban of Romania. This was for the final two years of the first Barroso Commission; Romania joined in 2007 and in 2009 the second Barroso commission was appointed. In the period 2007–2009, there was a dedicated Commissioner for multilingualism. There was an enormous window of opportunity at the time. European integration could have moved on to a deeper plane, one more relevant to the citizen. It is tragic that this opportunity, due to lack of vision in the leadership of the Commission, was not taken.

With the specific brief of contributing towards the development of EU multilingualism policy, I joined the DGT as a seconded national expert at this time, in September 2007. A Portuguese colleague, Anabela Pereira, edited an internal journal called *DGT Info*, which appeared every two months. It encouraged thinking about the whole area of language and identity in Europe, and about the crucially important area of how language policy could contribute to European integration, by strengthening a European identity, in harmony with national and regional identities. As we know, human beings have multiple identities, and there is no necessary contradiction between having strong regional, national and European identities. Such a strengthened European identity would not be in any way directed against countries outside of Europe. Europe would be more efficient if people felt that they are Europeans as well as French/Germans/Italians etc., and that they should cooperate more with their fellow Europeans. A European "*wir-Gefühl*" [we-feeling], as they say in German.

As soon as I arrived at the Commission, Anabela Pereira asked me to write an article for *DGT Info*, which I did right away. I wrote many articles and book reviews about the various aspects of multilingualism, including improved language learning, and the possible contribution of language policy to strengthening a European identity, multilingualism and language learning/language diversity – this whole area – for the eight years I was there. I also reviewed books calling for some possible role for Esperanto to be considered, particularly in the improvement of language learning. Unfortunately, the many ideas we developed did not reach decision-makers, and developments went in precisely the opposite direction. The new Cypriot Commissioner, Androulla Vassiliou, still retained multilingualism in 2009, but only as one of a number of responsibilities – she had culture, education and youth and multilingualism. She had to look after many other areas in addition to multilingualism, but it was still present, there was a unit dealing with multilingualism. It was no longer in the DGT – in the translation area – but in the cultural and educational area. The European Commission published a *"Communication on Multilingualism,"* and in October 2009 set up the European Civil Society Platform for Multilingualism/ECSPM.

When the ECSPM was set up, the Commission representative said, "we intend to do a report in two years about the views of the NGOs and non-governmental views about multilingualism to produce a further Commission communication on multilingualism, in 2011." Unfortunately, the idea was dropped, probably due to the action of some conservative forces within the Commission. The platform for multilingualism continued to work, and still exists, though it is no longer financed by the Commission. It produced an agreed report in 2011. It was submitted to the Commission, and it had some very progressive ideas. The report drew attention to the growing dominance of English within the EU institutions, the passivity of the institutions in accepting this as being somehow inevitable, and the harm this was doing to multilingualism. The Commission did not even copy the report to national ministries of education.

The report's first proposal in the educational area was on the need for practical experiments to test which second language most encourages subsequent language study. The proposal was to select language classes from around Europe, using different first foreign languages, and then objectively test achievement in the second foreign language. It was proposed to include Esperanto as a first foreign language, as this had been tested in the UK "Springboard for languages/S2L" programme in 2006–2011. The S2L programme taught children in four primary schools a small amount of Esperanto, not as an end in itself, but with two objectives: to raise language awareness and to prepare pupils for subsequent language study.

It was aimed in particular at those who are less linguistically talented. In each age cohort there are about 20 per cent who are really good at foreign languages and can pick up them up easily. There are, however, the other 80 per cent, the vast majority, whose talents are in other areas rather than in learning languages. The S2L programme found that a short course in Esperanto can help convince the 80 per cent that they may have more language learning talent than they realise. They could then begin to learn any third language with an expectation of success rather than of failure, and that can make all the difference.

This idea could become a game changer in improving language learning in general, and thus strengthening multilingualism. The Commission came round to financing a similar project through Erasmus+ in Croatia, Slovenia and Bulgaria in 2018 and 2019. It is called the "Multilingualism accelerator," or MLA, the brainchild of the late Zlatko Tišljar, a Croatian who did a lot of academic study on improving language learning, and on word frequency in actual use. He distilled Esperanto down to its most frequent 450 roots or morphemes – the equivalent of 2,000 words in other languages, due to Esperanto's very streamlined structure. However, as the course was designed for children aged eight to nine, he reduced the material further to 250 morphemes He discovered that concentrating on a smaller amount of learning material but mastering it so well that it becomes second nature to the learners, will have them actively using the new language much faster.

Tišljar and I had a disagreement on one occasion, and I have to say he was right. I did an Irish language version of a book written by a Slovak friend for Slovak learners of Esperanto. Tišljar was unimpressed by this book because he said it gives too much vocabulary for beginners, over 1,000 words. He said that this approach used a lot of time to learn words that are rarely used, and that this time could be more profitably used in mastering words which are essential to all communication, words such as "can," "could," "will," "would," "need," "want to" and their negative and interrogative forms.

The most revolutionary aspect of the MLA approach was that the programme was taught successfully by five professional primary-school teachers, none of whom spoke any Esperanto, initially. They were teaching in Croatia, Bulgaria and Slovenia, and they only needed one week of training to be able to teach the MLA programme. During that week, they learned the basic grammar of

Esperanto and its most common words. The MLA approach was an unqualified success: the children enjoyed the course and quickly began to use the new language actively, the teachers enjoyed teaching it, and the parents were very happy to see their children making such rapid progress.

This innovative approach has implications for language teaching all over Europe. For instance, in Ireland, Irish is obligatory from the beginning of primary school until the Baccalaureate. Therefore, from the age of four to the age of 17–18, everybody studies Irish, but the results are disappointing. About 30 per cent reach the targets, and about 70 per cent who study Irish for 12 years or more, never do. This convinces them that they have no talent for learning languages, so they do not even try to learn other languages. Introducing into this equation just a few weeks of Esperanto would be difficult, due to the lack of knowledge and strong prejudice which surround this language. Nevertheless, if irrational objections can be overcome, introducing the basic grammar and most frequent morphemes of Esperanto, with tests at the end where most learners will get close to 100 per cent, could give learners a rare psychological boost. It could be useful to Irish children learning Irish, or French, or to children across Europe learning English or any other language. They would start with a language that has no exceptions and was specifically designed to be easy to learn – the propaedeutic method.

This approach is widely adopted in other areas: for instance, when learning to swim, one begins at the shallow end of the pool; and skiing begins on the gentle slopes. To learn languages, by contrast, we tend to plunge into a new language with all its exceptions and exceptions to the exceptions; with vocabulary and phonemes that are entirely unfamiliar to learners. Then there are the irregular verbs, usually the most common verbs, which need to be learned before the learner has had the opportunity to grasp the basic structure of the regular verb. Irish has just 11 irregular verbs, but they include "say," "catch," "be," "do," "get," "eat," "give," "come," "go," "see," "hear" – words one needs to use all the time.

Returning to the ECSPM, the majority did not favour Esperanto, but were open-minded enough to propose exploring which first foreign language would most encourage subsequent language study, while not irrationally excluding Esperanto, as happens too often.

One further point on strange attitudes within DGT: when I joined it, there was a Lithuanian, two Italians and I who spoke Esperanto fluently. The four of us took to meeting for coffee once a week and chatting in Esperanto. This would have been the first time that many DGT linguists were exposed to fluent Esperanto in use, by colleagues from the south, the east and the west of Europe. The reaction of some, however, went in a different direction. Some joked: "We have 23 official languages in the EU, but that is not enough multilingualism for some colleagues. They wish to add a further language: Esperanto!"

[But you don't see a trend towards multilingualism in the EU...]

No, since 2007 the unfortunate trend is in the opposite direction. The second Barroso Commission weakened the position already by making multilingualism a mere part of a portfolio. When it was created as a separate portfolio in 2007, I thought it was a new dawn, and that there was a new understanding of the importance of language politically and emotionally for European integration. With hindsight, it appears that the Commission had to find something for the new Bulgarian and Romanian commissioners, whose countries joined the EU in 2007, so they invented a multilingualism portfolio. Unfortunately, though he worked hard in this area, the commissioner appointed, Orban, had no deep understanding of the potential political implications of his work. This was already apparent when he appointed his cabinet: a French chef de cabinet, a German deputy chef de cabinet, an Italian to keep Italy on board, and a Portuguese because Commission President Barroso was Portuguese. The last person appointed to the cabinet, a Finn whose first language is Swedish, was the only cabinet member with any expertise in the area. Multilingualism weakened under the second Barroso Commission and disappeared under the Juncker Commission in 2014. Europe moved away from multilingualism and towards English monolingualism, further and further in precisely the wrong direction.

The EU started with the Coal and Steel Community, so the economic area was always central. With the EEC/ European Economic Community, when Ireland joined in 1973, the economy remained central. Gradually non-economic areas began to develop, but there are those working in the EU institutions who feel that it's only about economic integration, that the economy is the only thing that matters. They forget that European integration concerns

The status of multilingualism in the European Commission 41

citizens, human beings, not just consumers. The economy will always remain an important element, probably the most important element, but it should not be the only element. The overall work on European integration has given too much emphasis to the economy, perhaps understandably. It has neglected other important realms, however, and because of this, when citizens get a chance to vote, they often vote against further European integration. This was seen in the referendums on the constitutional treaty in France and the Netherlands in 2005. Ireland has had nine referendums on EU integration, twice the citizens voted against. They felt left behind because the economic work had become very complex and bureaucratic. They no longer knew what "Brussels" was actually doing. It appears to the citizen to be some very complex economic work that few people understand. There was a joke in Ireland at the time of the referendum on the Single European Act, that "it is called the Single European Act because not a single European understands it!"

For instance, to look at a different area, though linked. In 2012, the European Citizens' Initiative/ECI was introduced as a new instrument to allow citizens to make proposals for consideration by the European Commission if the proposal had at least 1 million signatures. A further condition, added by the Commission, was that the signatures had to be collected within 12 months, with a minimum number in each of at least seven EU Member States. The proposal originally came from the European Parliament, which proposed 18 months to collect signatures, in a certain number of countries, but with no minimum number in each country. The Commission insisted on a year for signature collection, and a precise minimum number of signatures in each of at least seven countries. It is clear that the Commission's proposals were making it more and more difficult for citizens to have a say in Europe. The Commission went one step further than that: even if all the difficult conditions were fulfilled, the only obligation on the Commission is to study the proposal for three months, and, if rejecting it, to publish its reasons for rejecting. Critics of the Commission would say that the idea is to create the impression that citizens have an influence on policy development, while being very careful to prevent any real citizen influence.

I was appointed to the ECSPM (the platform for multilingualism) to represent the European Esperanto Union/EEU, the umbrella organisation of the national Esperanto associations in all 27 EU Member States. The role was quite separate from my work as a seconded national expert in the European Commission. The 29 organisations or networks concerned had been selected by the Commission from 62 applicant organisations. One of the criteria was ongoing activity in at least half of the EU Member States. The EEU was the only one out of 29 organisations to use Esperanto; the 28 others knew little about it and tended to be prejudiced against it. This is why there is no specific mention of Esperanto in the chapter on education in the 2011 ECSPM report to the Commission. We mentioned only the need for further research on which second language would be most likely to encourage subsequent language learning. However, there is a footnote about the S2L project in the UK, saying that it uses Esperanto to prepare for subsequent language learning, and therefore ought to be included.

In any case, the Esperanto movement decided to try to collect a million signatures across Europe for a recommendation that when citizens of different European countries want to sing the European anthem, Beethoven's Ninth, together, that they consider doing so in Esperanto. When the EU heads of state and government selected a European Anthem in 1985, they chose only music, and not the beautiful words of Schiller's "An die Freude," which have been translated into many other languages. The reason was to preserve the equality of the EU's official languages, and to avoid an anthem originally written in German, where all other versions would be mere translations of the German original. There is an original Esperanto version of the anthem, written by the Italian Umberto Broccatelli.[2]

When we met the then President of the European Parliament, Professor Jerzy Buzek, he was taken with the idea of signing the European Anthem in a neutral language, such as Esperanto or Latin. In line with the ECI regulations, we set up a committee with members in seven EU Member States. They included Nobel Prize winner Professor Reinhard Selten of Germany, Marco Panella of Italy, of the Radical Party, a long-time member of the European Parliament; together with French, Spanish, Polish and British colleagues ... from all the main countries we had somebody, and I was based in Belgium at that time. Our committee put forward the proposal and after consideration, the Commission issued a reply just before midnight on the final day. Despite considerable media

The status of multilingualism in the European Commission   43

interest, the Commission refused to register this proposal, on the grounds that it does not have the power to make such a recommendation, so we were not allowed to begin collecting signatures. This, despite the fact that we had a legal opinion from a European Parliament lawyer that the Commission does have the right to make such a proposal, because it has the task of representing the common European interest. I immediately wrote to the Commission, quoting the legal opinion we had received, and asked how the Commission could refute it. The Commission reply simply repeated its decision, adding that it did not have to justify its decisions.

In the Council of Ministers, each minister represents the interests of his/her member state. According to the treaties, the European Commission does not represent member states. In fact, each Commissioner has to swear that they will not take instructions from any national government, and that they will work for the common European interest. Many would argue that to enable citizens from different member states to sing the European anthem together in a common neutral language does contribute to the common European interest. However, the Commission clearly felt that this was dangerous territory, as it refused even to discuss their decision. We appealed to the European Ombudsman, who agreed with the Commission, but also gave no supporting arguments. Having thought about this a lot over the years, it appears to me that there is a lack of awareness in decision-makers. There is an appreciable gap between them and the academic area, where so much work has been undertaken. Decision-makers tend to be so busy with day-to-day work that they do not have time to study the academic work in the area, and so they are often unaware of it. This is a systemic weakness in decision-making at EU level.

5 Has a role for Esperanto ever been considered by the European Parliament?
A. In April 2004, there was a vote in the European Parliament, on the Dell'Alba Report, which slightly touched on Esperanto. Gianfranco Dell'Alba MEP was an Italian politician who was asked to draft a report about multilingualism in the European Parliament. He prepared his report, and inserted a sentence that the European Parliament should also consider *whether* a neutral language like Esperanto could make a contribution to strengthening

multilingualism in the Parliament. This proposal was voted out by the cultural-education committee, by 12 to 10.

It was a left-right split – the socialists, greens, communists, liberals, everybody left of centre, all voted to retain the reference to Esperanto. The right wing, both Christian Democrats and the far right, voted to remove any reference to Esperanto. An Irish Green MEP, Patricia McKenna, then collected the necessary signatures of 40 MEPs to have the reference re-inserted, which then had to be voted on in plenary. It was voted out again in plenary, by a show of hands – roughly 57 per cent against and 43 per cent in favour. Again, it was a similar left-right split, but the paradoxical thing was that, when this vote was taken, there were just two members of the European Parliament who spoke fluent Esperanto, Małgorzata Handzlik (Polish) and Ludmila Novak (Slovene). Both were members of the Christian Democrat Party, the EPP. Their party was voting against this reference to Esperanto, but both voted in favour, of course. I had long discussions with the two MEPs concerned at the time, and both said that their party leadership did not want any discussion about the idea, and that they "did not want any discussion of why they did not want to discuss it." Rather similar to the Commission's refusal to justify its decision regarding an ECI on the European Anthem.

This brings us to the psychological phenomenon which Professor Claude Piron called *"l'ignorance ignorée"* [ignored ignorance]. It is not just that people know nothing about this; it's even worse: they do not even know that there is anything to be known about this. Esperanto has existed for five generations, it has developed its own very rich original literature, a huge translated literature – of well over 10,000 literary works translated from most of the main languages of the world. Almost every day a new book is published in Esperanto, and there is a lively music scene. Many people do not realise that there are native speakers, drama, poetry etc., and that Esperanto has been in use intensively by a small but worldwide community for five generations. So they think that the whole thing is a waste of time, and do not take it seriously. Many decision-makers are blinded by lack of knowledge, and by deep prejudice based on that lack of knowledge. It appears that the concept of an inter-ethnic language as a viable option is as taboo in western society as was that of the market economy in the former Soviet Union.

On 12 March 2002, the question of a possible role for Esperanto was also addressed by Neil Kinnock, then Vice-President of the European Commission, in a reply to a question in the European Parliament. His reply could be summed up as rejecting a role for Esperanto as a relay language in interpretation on a number of questionable grounds, the most striking of which is "recourse to a language that is not used in everyday life would run the risk of not being able to convey the full range of messages and ideas communicated during meetings." This reply displays a regrettable lack of awareness by Mr Kinnock, and the officials who drafted his reply, of the extent to which Esperanto is in actual use on all continents. Such a language can no longer be seen as artificial. It begins as artificial, like a test tube baby, but becomes a child like any other child.

Commentary

The issue of a more prominent role for language policy in the EU's political framework dovetails with the question of the EU's areas of competence, itself the embodiment of the *raison d'être* of the Union. Originally conceived in the aftermath of World War II as a Coal and Steel Community grounded in the mutual interest to prevent future conflicts, the bloc gradually evolved into the economic community of the four freedoms we know today, namely the freedom of people, goods, capital and services across invisible borders.

The emphasis on the economy, as noted by Ó Riain, grew perhaps as a "natural" outcome of this primary goal. This "natural" requires qualification, as some would argue that the EU can be perceived as an "empire" of sorts (see Behr & Stivachtis 2016), as well as that the USA played a key part in shaping the EU from the very beginning (see Phillipson 2016). The Treaty establishing the European Coal and Steel Community, of 1951, features three clusters of reasons to justify the creation of the community, namely peace, a notion of shared destiny (more in Chapter 5) and the economy. Yet the over 300 pages of the document focus almost exclusively on this third cluster, with the common market showcased in every section (see Leal 2021, 128). Later, the then European Community's turn towards neoliberalism, deregulation and globalisation, starting in the 1980s, underlined the bloc's increasing economic emphasis.

Yet with the Treaty of Maastricht in 1993 and other "nation-building" initiatives mentioned in Chapter 1 (including the introduction of EU symbols), the EU also explicitly sought to foster its civic dimension and its integration through different approaches. While the symbols (particularly the flag and the anthem) constituted a more culturalist attempt to "inculcate" in the citizenry a notion of European identity, Maastricht was underpinned by the construct of European citizenship to achieve the same goal. But regardless of the approach, the apocryphal quote by Jean Monnet, which some attribute to Hélène Ahrweiler, says it all: "If we were to do it all over again, we should begin with culture" (see Collins 1996, 13; Kraus 2008, 43; Lamour & Lorentz 2019, 357: Leal 2021, 129).

The corollary of this conflicted scenario – in which the economy invariably takes centre stage, but issues of culture and identity cannot be swept under the carpet – is the distribution of areas of competence between the member states and the EU. As shown in Table 2.2, language policy does not lie within the EU's jurisdiction, neither as an exclusive, nor as a shared or supporting competence. The EU's areas of competence are stipulated in the treaties; any changes would require treaty change, for which unanimity among the member states would be necessary. Yet, for the same reasons that prevent a number of EU member states from signing and/or ratifying the European Charter for Regional or Minority Languages – a conundrum addressed in Chapter 1 – achieving consensus among all member states on an arrangement to share competence with the EU in the area of language policy is well-nigh impossible. This is known as the principle of conferral: EU countries confer certain competences upon the EU through consensus decisions enshrined in the treaties.

The only way for the EU to take action in areas that fall beyond its remit is through the principle of subsidiarity which, along with the principle of proportionality, complements the principle of conferral. "Subsidiarity" means that the EU is allowed to act only in those areas which fall outside its exclusive competence (such as language policy) when its action will be more effective than action taken locally. "Proportionality" means that any such actions taken by the EU on grounds of subsidiarity may not go beyond what is strictly necessary to achieve the objectives of the treaties.

Table 2.2 EU areas of competence

Exclusive competences	Shared competences	Supporting competences	Special competences
Only the EU can legislate	Both EU and member states can legislate	Member states legislate and EU supports, coordinates and complements	"Special" permission for EU to go beyond treaties
Competition rules Customs union Marine plants and animals Monetary policy Trade	Agriculture Consumer protection Economic, social and territorial cohesion Employment Energy Environment Fisheries Fundamental rights Home affairs Justice Migration Public health (for the aspects defined in Article 168 of the Treaty on the Functioning of the European Union) Research Single market Social affairs Space Trans-European networks Transport	Administrative cooperation Civil protection Culture Education Industry Public health Tourism Training, youth and sport	Coordination of economic and employment policies Definition and implementation of the Common Foreign and Security Policy The 'flexibility clause' – which under strict conditions enables the EU to take action outside its normal areas of responsibility

Source: https://ec.europa.eu/info/about-european-commission/what-european-commission-does/law/areas-eu-action_en

This means that, by default, the EU's jurisdiction regarding language policy is limited to the symbolic level.[3] However, it could engender more robust language policies by resorting to subsidiarity and conforming to proportionality – at least legally speaking. Any draft legislative acts proposed in the area of language policy would nevertheless have to be approved by each national parliament; if at least one third of the national parliaments decided that the draft legislative act in question did not comply with the principle of subsidiarity, the proposal would have to be reviewed. If 55 per cent of the ministers in the Council of the European Union or a simple majority in the European Parliament confirmed this non-compliance, the draft would have to be withdrawn altogether (see Leal 2021, 52).[4]

The legal mechanisms to introduce supranational language policy are thus in place, but as they currently stand, they by no means facilitate any initiatives. The adoption of concrete EU-wide language policies would require not only a bold step on the part of the EU, potentially encroaching upon member states' areas of competence, but also an almost utopian willingness to comply on the part of the member states (see Leal 2021, 52).[5]

This legal quandary provides the backdrop for the European Citizens' Initiative mentioned earlier in this chapter, "Minority SafePack," and for Ó Riain's discussion about a role for a planned language in the EU (more in what follows). Whenever the question of language policy arises, the Commission's default reaction is to dismiss it as it lies outside its jurisdiction. There is little appetite to go into language questions, as noted by Ó Riain and revealed in my recent interview with the current custodians of multilingualism in the EU, DGT (see Leal 2021, 207–214).

This begs the question of the role and institutional standing of multilingualism in the Commission. During the brief period in which it had its own portfolio, multilingualism enjoyed some limelight in its Commissioner's, Leonard Orban, speeches and articles. Though some – including Ó Riain – argue that Orban did not push hard enough for reform and remained constrained within symbolic politics, it is undeniable that having a portfolio and unit dedicated to multilingualism is better than having none. Yet bringing this portfolio back to life seems off the table now that multilingualism is under the auspices of DGT. Creating a unit to monitor and foster multilingualism within DGT would be a small and urgent step towards giving multilingualism the standing that would be expected of one of the pillars of the EU, as well as towards fulfilling the policy-making powers bestowed upon DGT. This step could profit from engaging the existing Commission's representations in the member states,[6] so that the multilingualism unit within DGT does not remain a centralised entity, distant from the realities of the member states – which, when it comes to language policies, practices and ideologies, can be widely different. This would be the closest thing possible to establishing an EU agency for language policy and planning without having to undergo the bureaucratic procedures of treaty change and achieving unanimity among the member states (see Leal 2021, 182, 186).

As argued in Chapter 1, part of the member states' reluctance to address language policy at the supranational level stems from a concern over the unity of the state – both politically and ideologically. Let us not forget here that the notion of "national language," as a unifying and artificial construct, was born with the nation state in the aftermath of the French Revolution. A common language is still traditionally perceived as a prerequisite for a *demos*, or a public sphere (in the Habermasian [1962] sense of *Öffentlichkeit*). Through this prism, any recognition or rights granted to speakers of languages other than the national language(s) could thus pose a threat to the integrity of the very nation. Indeed, an influential line of thought links John Stuart Mill, Karl Deutsch, Jürgen Habermas and Dieter Grimm in the belief that a common political culture, grounded in a common language, is a prerequisite for any democratic community (Steeg & Risse 2010; Kraus 2011, 21–22; Wright 2011; Leal 2021, 133).

This notion is already controversial at the national level in today's EU, where multilingualism is becoming the norm, not least through the freedom of movement across borders and the multiple waves of immigration into the bloc. At the transnational level, establishing a common political culture grounded in a common language – a public sphere, as it were – becomes a herculean task. Yet do we need a common language in the EU for an EU-wide public sphere to emerge?

Recent research shows that there is a burgeoning European public sphere despite political, linguistic and geographical borders (Steeg & Risse 2010). What is more, recent studies also reveal that language forms a contingent – albeit important – layer in our "repertoires of different identities" (Blommaert 2006, 245). To concur with Ó Riain in the above interview, these identity layers do not compete but rather harmonise with each other. They are language-bound inasmuch as language plays a pivotal part in virtually all of these layers – be they supranational, national, regional, local, etc. However, this does not preclude different identity layers from being shared across languages, as seems to be the case in the EU (see Leal 2021, 138).

The issue of our identity repertoires and the part that language plays in them goes hand in hand with the question of a role for a planned language like Esperanto in the EU. Gianfranco Dell'Alba, mentioned by Ó Riain in this chapter's interview, wrote the following in his 2004 report on multilingualism commissioned by European Parliament:

> ...on the basis of an underlying desire to preserve the cultural and linguistic diversity of the European Union, the rapporteur would like, in conclusion, to raise (...) the idea of promoting a neutral pivot language such as Esperanto. A language such as this could encourage cross-cultural communication, while offering an alternative to the evergrowing preponderance of certain of the current languages, without, however, endangering the linguistic heritage which is one of Europe's most precious assets.
>
> (Dell'Alba 2004, 12)

As noted by Ó Riain, this mention was narrowly voted out but can still be read in the final sections of Dell'Alba's report. A common justification for a blank refusal of Esperanto in the most varied contexts is precisely the identity route. Many see Esperanto as devoid of culture, music, literature and history, which is a common misconception, as revealed in the interview. What it does lack is a territorial – and hence political – basis, which in turn often erroneously translates as a lack of culture. The dictum *cuius regio, eius religio*, whose "natural" continuation is *cuius regio, eius lingua* (see Kraus 2008, 86), underpins the "one nation, one language" mentality which informs our notion of culture as well. Esperanto's lack of geographical and, hence, political boundedness acts as a double-edged sword. One the one hand, it makes it a politically

The status of multilingualism in the European Commission 51

neutral language, attached to no particular member state; its promotion accrues profits and prestige to no nation or nationalities. On the other hand, there is no nation behind it, pushing for its recognition and fostering its promotion.

In the recent Conference on the future of Europe, Esperanto featured in some of the most successful initiatives – not as an end in itself, but as a bridge to language learning. "The EU needs improved language learning," proposed by Ó Riain, was the most endorsed and the most commented on in the realm of education, culture, youth and sport, with 729 endorsements and 157 comments (Kantar Public 2022, 119), as well as the fifth most popular overall (out of over 16,000 proposals – see the Preface). Furthermore, 11 additional proposals approached multilingualism explicitly, with numerous others addressing minority languages and foreign language learning. These initiatives or proposals were gathered in the Conference's multilingual digital platform and are still accessible there.[7]

Though popular among the proposals submitted to the Conference's platform, language-related initiatives did not filter through to the "final outcome" of the Conference. Nor do they form part of the 49 proposals which resulted from the Conference and are currently being pushed by the European Parliament – including the possibility of treaty changes. This is probably because the multilingual digital platform constituted but one step in the Conference, based on which four panels, each containing 200 randomly selected EU citizens, drafted recommendations over three deliberative sessions. These recommendations were then sent to the Conference's executive board, made up of three representatives from the European Parliament, three from the Council of the EU and three from the Commission, along with observers. The executive board then reported to the so-called joint presidency, i.e., the presidents of the Parliament, the Council of the EU and the Commission (see European Union 2022 and n.d.).

As one would expect, a lot of "pick and choose" took place at each of these stages. Furthermore, although the citizen's panels – and presumably all involved in the drafting of recommendations and proposals in the later stages of the Conference – had access to "resources and experts on the topics" they "chose to discuss," it remains unclear who these experts were and whether information was provided on the different sides relevant to the debates in question (European Union n.d., 6). To make matters worse, the panel entrusted with the language-related proposals gathered in the multilingual platform were also responsible for all proposals pertaining to the following areas: stronger economy, social justice, jobs, youth, sport, culture, education and digital transformation (see European Union 2022 and n.d.).

Designed as an innovative mechanism to increase citizen participation in an EU riddled with charges of democratic deficit, the Conference on the future of Europe is a crucial step in the right direction. Yet as the question of language illustrates, the format chosen is not conducive to efficient, fair and transparent democratic debate. There are numerous strategies to reform the ECI so that the glitches outlined here no longer happen (see, e.g., Falanga 2018; Chilvers & Kearnes 2020; Fernández-Martínez, García-Espín and Jiménez-Sánchez 2020).[8] As this chapter's interview illustrates, the EU is in dire need of mechanisms to increase citizen participation, and this requires closer links between policy-makers and academia to ensure that these mechanisms reflect the state of the art in the relevant academic disciplines.

The need to bridge policy-making and academia in the EU features repeatedly in this book. It applies to multilingualism and planned languages as well. There is no shortage of academic work emphasising the importance of multilingualism and endorsing the potentially positive effect of a role for a planned language on different levels – financial, educational, cultural, political. From the perspective of language economics, François Grin, for example, shows that a multilingual world is both fairer and more prosperous (Grin 2010 and 2018). Back in 2005, he estimated that the dominance of English in Europe accrued €17 billion to the UK that year alone (and this is a "conservative" estimate – see Leal 2021, 148). The bottom line for Grin is that, regardless of how we perceive the importance of multilingualism or lack thereof, the dominance of any given national language leads to palpable, quantifiable injustices which cannot be ignored.

In a similar vein, different research projects financed by the Commission call for a more explicit focus on language policy. Take, for instance, the first key result of the MIME project "Mobility and inclusion in multilingual Europe," conducted between 2014–2018: "policies encouraging individual multilingualism and embracing societal multilingualism yield material and symbolic benefits that exceed their costs and are conducive to more fairness in society" (Conceição et al. 2018, 26). This conclusion echoes across similar projects on European multilingualism spanning a few decades.

However, as is the case with most scholarly debates in the humanities and social sciences, these views, albeit prevalent, are not consensual and meet with interesting opposition. One of the most noteworthy for the purposes of this book is Philippe Van Parijs's model of linguistic justice through English as the world's lingua franca. Predicated on comprehensive, high-quality and universally accessible English teaching around the globe, his model entails eventually lifting the territoriality principle which links – be it overtly or covertly – a particular language or languages to virtually all nations in the world, ultimately culminating in the disappearance of the 7,000 plus languages active today (see Van Parijs 2008, 2011 and 2015). In his words – and especially interestingly in our context in this book – his model might "tur[n] the whole planet into a large number of Republics of Ireland, with only vestiges of the local languages (...) and with a somewhat idiosyncratic way of pronouncing the lingua franca, now promoted to mother tongue status" (Van Parijs 2015, 242). We will come back to Van Parijs's model of linguistic justice in Chapter 4.

The issue of the lack of dialogue between politicians and decision-makers, on the one hand, and academia, on the other, is decisive – as noted by Ó Riain. Even though the EU has commissioned scholarly reports and studies on multilingualism, as well as directly engaged with language policy experts (see, e.g., European Commission 2011), policy remains a far cry from the state-of-the-art in academia. This raises important questions about the quality of EU policy-makers' decisions in the realm of language. No government would make decisions on, say, nuclear energy or the environment without relying on expert opinions and the latest developments in that particular field. Given the prominence of language as one of the pillars of the European project, relying on specialists in the area to inform decision-making should be a given. This takes us back to the need to create an institutional framework for language policy – an issue to which we will return repeatedly in what follows.

Notes

1 See Case T-646/13 and www.minoritysafepack.eu/ – last accessed in January 2023.
2 See www.youtube.com/watch?v=10L3Qmxd8bs and translations are available into 40 languages (see www.europo.eu/en/citizens-initiative, both links last accessed in February 2023.
3 For the development of the principle of subsidiarity in the West, see Kraus (2008, 183–188).
4 This is only a snapshot of the process which, in reality, has a few additional intricacies – see "Protocol No. 2 on the Application of the Principles of Subsidiarity and Proportionality" in the TFEU.
5 See Barbier (2018, 351, 352) for an appraisal of subsidiarity as an "illusory protection" to "placate the concerns of the Member States."
6 Each EU member state relies on a local Commission Representation, among whose tasks is "providing the Commission with political information and analysis" (see https://ec.europa.eu/info/about-european-commission/contact/representations-member-states_en – last accessed in October 2022). This would align with providing DGT with "political information and analysis" of relevant issues surrounding language policy and practice in the respective member state. These representations are usually staffed with a head of representation and around a dozen to two or three dozen officers in different areas, such as "political and economic monitoring," "press section," "communication section," etc.
7 Those under the rubric "Education, culture, youth and sport," among which are all language-related proposals, can be found here: https://futureu.europa.eu/processes/Education/f/36/proposals/1536 (last accessed in October 2022).
8 I would like to thank Fernando Varnier Borges and Dulce Lopes (Faculdade de Direito, University of Coimbra, Portugal) for recommending these sources.

References

Barbier, Jean-Claude. 2018. "European integration and the variety of languages: An awkward co-existence." In *The politics of multilingualism: Europeanisation, globalisation and linguistic governance*, edited by François Grin and Peter A. Kraus, 333–357. Amsterdam & Philadelphia: John Benjamins.
Behr, Hartmut, and Yannis A. Stivachtis. 2016. "European Union: An empire in new clothes?" In *Revisiting the European Union as empire*, edited by Hartmut Behr and Yannis A. Stivachtis, 1–16. Abingdon & New York: Routledge.

Blommaert, J. (2006) "Language policy and national identity." In *An introduction to language policy: Theory and method* edited by T. Ricento, 238–254. Oxford: Blackwell Publishing.

Buck, Tobias. 2006. "Romania's less than glittering prize." *Financial Times*, 1 November. https://web.archive.org/web/20110711045737/http://us.ft.com/ftgateway/superpage.ft?news_id=fto110120060255093038.

Chilvers, Jason, and Matthew Kearnes. 2020. "Remaking participation in science and democracy." *Science, Technology, & Human Values* 45 (3): 347–380.

Collins, Richard. 1996. "The North Atlantic cultural triangle: The Bermuda syndrom?" In *Difference and community: Canadian and European cultural perspectives*, edited by Peter Easingwood, Konrad Gross and Lynette Hunter, 13–26. Amsterdam & Atlanta: Rodopi.

Conceição et al., Manuel Célio. 2018. "Key results." In *Mobility and inclusion in multilingual Europe: The MIME Vademecum*, edited by François Grin, 26–27.

De Swaan, Abram. 1993. "The evolving European language system: A theory of communication potential." *International Political Science Review* 14 (3): 241–255.

Dell'Alba, Gianfranco. 2004. *A5-0153/2004*. Brussels: European Parliament.

European Commission. 2010. *Translation at the European Commission – a history*. Luxembourg: Office for Official Publications of the European Communities.

European Commission. 2011. "Lingua franca: Chimera or reality?"

European Union. n.d. "Conference on the future of Europe: European citizens' panels – panels' guide." https://futureu.europa.eu/rails/act ive_storage/blobs/eyJfcmFpbHMiOnsibWVzc2FnZSI6IkJBaHBBdm NhIiwiZXhwIjpudWxsLCJwdXIiOiJibG9iX2lkIn19--38b78b84d6d9a 508471bf5cc9a45a357c74ed4db/en21.pdf.

European Union. 2022. *Conference on the future of Europe: Report on the final outcome*. European Union: Brussels.

Falanga, R. 2018. "Critical trends of citizen participation in policy-making: Insights from Portugal." In *Changing Societies: Legacies and Challenges. Vol. II. Citizenship in Crisis* edited by M. C. Lobo, F. C. da Silva and J. P. Zúquete 295–318. Lisbon: Imprensa de Ciências Sociais.

Fernández-Martínez, José Luis, Patricia García-Espín, and Manuel Jiménez-Sánchez. 2020. "Participatory frustration: The unintended cultural effect of local democratic innovations." *Administration & Society* 52 (5): 718–748.

Grin, F. 2010. "Why multilingualism is affordable." *Seminario sobre lingua, sociedade i política en Galicia*, 1–15. Santiago de Compostela.

Habermas, Jürgen. 1962. *Strukturwandel der Öffentlichkeit. Untersuchungen zu einer Kategorie der bürgerlichen Gesellschaft.* Darmstadt & Neuwied: Luchterhand Verlag.

Kantar Public. 2022. *Multilingual digital platform of the Conference on the future of Europe.* Brussels: Kantar Public.

Kraus, Peter A. 2008. *A union of diversity: Language, identity and polity-building in Europe.* Cambridge: Cambridge University Press.

Kraus, Peter A. 2011. "Neither united nor diverse? The language issue and political legitimation in the European Union." In *Linguistic diversity and European democracy*, edited by Anne Lise Kjaer and Silvia Adamo, 17–34. Farnham: Ashgate.

Lamour, Christian, and Nathalie Lorentz. 2019. "'If I were to do it all over again, should I begin with culture?' The European integration from a cultural perspective in a multi-national Grand Duchy." *Journal of Contemporary European Studies* 27 (3): 357–374.

Leal, Alice. 2021. *English and translation in the European Union: Unity and multiplicity in the wake of Brexit.* Abingdon & New York: Routledge.

Phillipson, Robert. 2016. "Linguistic imperialism of and in the European Union." In *Revisiting the European Union as empire*, by Hartmut Behr and Yannis A. Stivachtis, 134–163. Abingdon & New York: Routledge.

Steeg, Marianne van de, and Thomas Risse. 2010. "The emergence of a European Community of communication: Insights from empirical research on the Europeanization of public spheres." *KFG Working Paper Series* 15: 1–30.

Van Parijs, Philippe. 2008. "Linguistic diversity as curse and as by-product." In *Respecting linguistic diversity in the European Union*, edited by Xabier Arzoz, 17–46. Amsterdam & Philadelphia: John Benjamins.

Van Parijs, Philippe. 2011. *Linguistic justice for Europe and for the world.* Oxford: Oxford University Press.

Van Parijs, Philippe. 2015. "The ground floor of the world: On the socio-economic consequences of linguistic globalization." In *Language policy and political economy: English in a global context*, edited by Thomas Ricento, 231–251. Oxford: Oxford University Press.

Wright, Sue. 2011. "Democracy, communities of communication and the European Union." In *Linguistic diversity and European democracy*, edited by Anne Lise Kjaer and Silvia Adamo, 35–56. Farnham: Ashgate.

3 The European Commission and English as a "lingua franca"

Introductory remarks

The European Union (EU) has 24 official and working languages, namely Bulgarian, Croatian, Czech, Danish, Dutch, English, Estonian, Finnish, French, German, Greek, Hungarian, Irish, Italian, Latvian, Lithuanian, Maltese, Polish, Portuguese, Romanian, Slovak, Slovenian, Spanish and Swedish. Their status as official *and* working languages is enshrined in the treaties and precludes the possibility of a *de jure* pecking order among them. Yet, *de facto*, today English is the EU's lingua franca of sorts. The interview with Seán Ó Riain below offers a description of the language practices, policies and ideologies of the European Commission (particularly of the Directorate-General for Translation – DGT); a critical discussion of the dominance of English and the *modus operandi* of the Commission's language services; an appraisal of the current role of French in these settings; a debate on whether there is a need for a lingua franca in the EU and, if so, whether English is a suitable candidate; as well as a presentation of alternatives to the current, largely monolingual *modus operandi* grounded in English.

Below is the body of EU primary law pertaining to language policy. In a nutshell, it confers the status of both official *and* working language upon all 24 EU languages. Two important points here. First, the legislation in Table 3.1 is qualified by further articles in the same document. Regulation 1958/1, for instance, includes additional articles that give the EU institutions free rein to stipulate their own language policy.

DOI: 10.4324/9781003342069-3

Table 3.1 Overview of language policy in EU primary law

European Economic Community regulation no. 1 (15 April 1958)	"The official languages and the working languages of the institutions of the Community shall be Dutch, French, German and Italian." [Today this list contains 24 languages.]
Article 24 – Treaty on the Functioning of the European Union	"Every citizen of the Union may write to any of the institutions or bodies (…) in one of the languages mentioned in Article 55(1) of the Treaty on European Union [TEU] and have an answer in the same language."
Article 55 – The final provisions of the Treaty on European Union	[The treaty was] "drawn up in a single original in the Dutch, French, German, and Italian languages, all four texts being equally authentic." [Today this list contains 24 languages.]
Article 22 – EU Charter of Fundamental Rights	"The Union shall respect cultural, religious and linguistic diversity."

Second, the Irish language only attained its full status of official and working language on 1 January 2022. Upon Ireland's accession, Irish was declared a "treaty language," i.e., only primary law was published in it. In the wake of Malta's accession in 2004 and the recognition of Maltese as an official and working language, Ireland requested that Irish, too, be granted the same status – albeit retroactively. Malta's accession triggered similar motions from other language groups in addition to the Irish, given that one of the two Maltese official languages, namely English, was already an EU official language upon Malta's accession. Consequently, it was the first time that a member state had a second and exclusive language recognised by the EU as an official and working language. Unlike the other contenders – such as Catalan – Irish received a favourable decision from the EU but was placed in derogation between 2007 and 2022. In fact, Maltese had

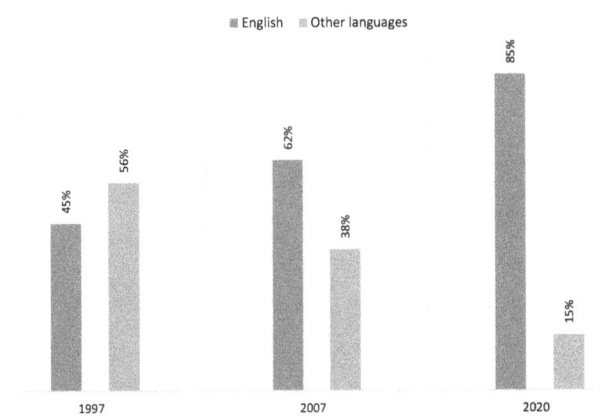

Figure 3.1 Drafting statistics at the Commission

Source: European Commission (2009 and 2020b). See also Sandrelli (2018, 64) and Cliffe (2019).

also been placed under derogation for three years in 2004. This was due mostly to a lack of translators and interpreters in these languages.

However superficial the articles displayed in Table 3.1 may be, they lay out clearly that there can be no hierarchy among the official languages, at least officially. Unofficially, there is an indisputable abyss between all other official languages and English, today the EU's *ad hoc* lingua franca of sorts, as the statistics above and below illustrate.

Figures 3.3. and 3.4 show the results of surveys conducted among Commission staff, whereas Figures 3.1 and 3.2 reveal the dominance of English in terms of drafting. Drafting processes vary across the institutions, as reported, for instance, by Sue Wright (2007), Joxerramon Bengoetxea (2011), William Robinson (2014) and Jean-Claude Barbier (2018). In her research at the Parliament, Wright (2007, 155), for example, reports that some of her respondents struggle with the drafting process because "much of the preparatory paper work [*sic*] [is] only available in English" and "drafting and negotiation [are] increasingly in English." While they emphasise that all documents are eventually made

60 *The European Commission and English as a "lingua franca"*

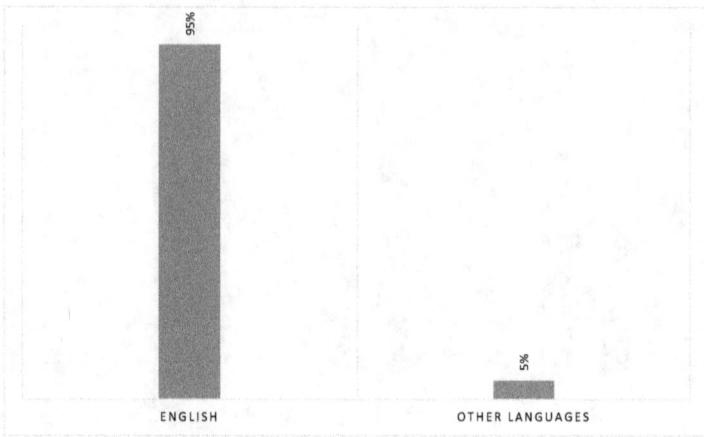

Figure 3.2 Legal drafting statistics
Source: Barbier (2018, 337).

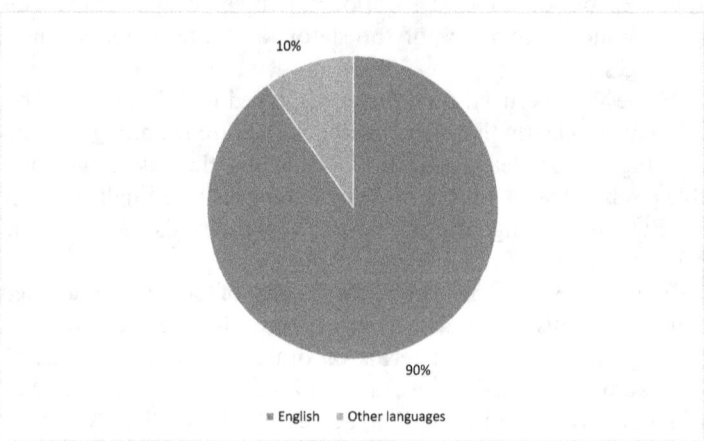

Figure 3.3 Choice of main drafting language in the Commission in 2009
Source: Robinson (2014, 194).

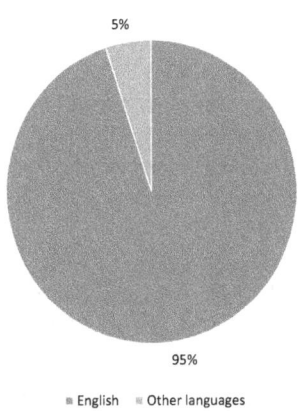

Figure 3.4 Most used language among Commission staff when performing their duties in 2016

Source: See, e.g., recruitment notices PE/219/S and PE/200/S.

available in all relevant languages, "[a]ll the important consultation, negotiation and dealing happens" in more informal settings and gatherings, predominantly in English, which is systematically perceived as the (often lowest but only) common denominator (Wright 2007, 156).

A sidenote here. This phenomenon of the automatic compromise on English in multilingual settings is explained by Philippe Van Parijs's "maxi-min" principle. In a nutshell, we tend to speak the "language (...) best known by the member of [our] audience who knows it least well" or the language of "maximal minimal competence" (Van Parijs 2011, 14). In a room where 24 people speak, say, Portuguese fluently, the arrival of one, say, Spanish or Italian speaker will prompt everyone to switch to English, even though many of these 25 are not proficient in it. Relying on intercomprehension (even for languages as close as Spanish and Portuguese) or on whispered interpretation would rarely come into question in these settings; yet these alternatives to the "maxi-min" principle would increase the quality of conversation significantly.

In any case, the dominance of English in the informal settings surrounding drafting in the EU is mirrored in the drafting itself, resulting in a majority of original texts in English. This, in turn, generates a translation regime which is geared towards English. In Table 3.2, we see François Grin's translation regimes adapted to the EU context. The EU's official translation regime is panarchic, with 24 official languages enjoying the same status, and all legally binding documents being available in all 24 – in compliance with Article 248 of the final provisions of the Treaty establishing the European Community (today Article 55 of the final provisions of the TEU – see Table 3.1),

However, the panarchic regime is only in place for binding documents and even then, 95 per cent of originals are in English – a dominance which cannot be erased or compensated for by the existence of translations. In those few cases in which binding documents are drafted in languages other than English, they may be translated via the triple symmetrical relay regime, whereby pivot languages (in this case, three, but it could be fewer or more) are used to bridge less common language pairs – say, Irish-Maltese or Estonian-Greek.

Yet binding documents constitute but one text type in the EU. Most other text types follow the monarchic regime, whereby drafting takes places in English and no translation is available. In some cases, the oligarchic regime may be in place as well, whereby information is made available in English and French, more rarely German as well. The reader may recall that these are the EU's unofficial "procedural languages" – a category that enjoys no legal backing whatsoever but which, nevertheless, is mentioned repeatedly in communications from different EU institutions, bodies and agencies (see, e.g., European Commission 2009, 3; Leal 2021, 51).

In what follows, Ó Riain is critical of the turn to English not only as main drafting language, but also as the language that dominates conversation – even in units such as DGT, the current custodians of multilingualism in the EU (see Chapter 2). Ó Riain warns that an "English-only Europe" – which is the title of Robert Phillipson's polemical 2003 book also mentioned in the interview below – runs the risk of alienating the citizenry and exacerbating an identification crisis already in full swing. Phillipson's work, fiery and controversial as it may be for many, points to undeniable injustices and discrepancies in the EU's use of languages, particularly regarding the unchecked, unofficial and especially seemingly *ad hoc* hegemony of English.

Table 3.2 EU translation regimes

Translation regime	Status	Use
Panarchic (24 official and working languages)	Official (sanctioned in the treaties)	Most legally binding documents are drafted in English and translated into the other 23 languages
Triple symmetrical relay (24 official and working languages with three pivot languages)	Semi-official (informally mentioned in official sources, e.g., European Parliament n.d.)	The small proportion of legally binding documents drafted in languages other than English are translated into the other 23 (often via a pivot language)
Monarchic* (one working language)	Unofficial (not mentioned in official sources, possibly in breach of EU legislation – e.g., §21 and §22 of the Charter of Fundamental Rights)	Most non-legally binding texts are drafted in English and are not translated
Oligarchic* (three working languages)	Semi-official (informally mentioned in official sources, e.g., European Commission 2009)	The small proportion of non-legally binding texts drafted in languages other than English are translated into English and sometimes French, rarely German

Source: The first column was taken from Grin (2008). Adapted from Leal (2021, 95).

* In Grin's terminology, the languages pertaining to these regimes are both official and working languages. Yet the EU's *de jure* "panarchic" system seems permanent. I therefore suggest adapting the "monarchic" and "oligarchic" regimes to entail working languages only – or rather "procedural" languages.

Some of Phillipson's most vociferous critics include representatives of the ELF (English as a lingua franca) paradigm, which is also mentioned briefly by Ó Riain in what follows. ELF proponents take a descriptive approach to the phenomenon of the spread of English among speakers of different languages who find themselves in multilingual settings. Their empirical findings, though riddled with accusations of elitism and lack of touch with multilingualism beyond academia, reveal that ELF can be considered "norm-developing," to use Braj Kachuru's terminology, thus placing it on a par – in status – with "native" (or "inner-circle") varieties of English (Kachru, Kachru & Nelson 2006; Seidlhofer 2011).[1]

One of the main contentions of the ELF paradigm is that ELF is a *sui generis* language use, based not on fixed, *a priori* rules, but rather negotiated *ad hoc* in each communicative situation according to each speaker's – especially linguistic – background. This fluidity and hybridity, in turn, prevent ELF from claiming variety status, in the spirit of the World Englishes movement and the celebration of "outer-circle" Englishes (see endnote 1 below).

Another pillar of ELF is the radical rethinking of the notion of "mistake" in English. Its advocates propose that ELF need not be taken against inner-circle norms – very much in line with liberation linguistics and the rupture with monocentric approaches to English seen, for instance, within the World Englishes paradigm, too. Barbara Seidlhofer (one of the protagonists of ELF), for example, insists that if sizeable communities of speakers systematically say "informations," then surely the use must be deemed correct. This is relevant in the EU context because EU jargon (nicknamed "Brussels-speak" or "Euro-English," among many other less flattering epithets) is known for including deviations from "standard" English. Jeremy Gardner, former senior translation at the European Court of Auditors, has famously compiled a guide of such "misuses" (such as "actually" instead of "currently"), much to the discontent of ELF thinkers (Gardner 2016 – see Jenkings & Cogo 2010).

From within the World Englishes paradigm, Marko Modiano has also endeavoured to describe what he calls "Euro-English" and has pushed for it to be recognised as the EU's sole lingua franca. Unlike ELF proponents, Modiano does not focus on the variability of Euro-English and, instead, highlights the common features that, in his view, grant Euro-English the status of an outer-circle (hence norm-developing) variety of English in its own right (Modiano 2009, 2017).

Both the ELF paradigm and thinkers such as Modiano perceive English as a neutral instrument of communication – an issue taken up in this chapter's interview. Especially within the ELF paradigm, the notion that English is *not* a neutral vessel, that it is *not* deprived of cultural and ideological layers and that it leaves an *imprint* on its speakers and their languages is contested virulently (see, e.g., Jenkins 2007, Seidlhofer 2011).

Can English be a neutral instrument of communication, a lingua franca *sensu stricto*, coloured almost entirely by the cultural and ideological markers of its speakers' mother tongues, as defended by ELF advocates? In the wake of Brexit, can it be a politically neutral language and hence the best-suited contender to become the EU's official lingua franca, as proposed, for example, by Modiano? To answer these questions, we first need to ask ourselves (1) what a lingua franca is, (2) whether national languages can be neutral instruments and, finally, (3) whether the EU needs a lingua franca in the first place.

(1) Traditionally, a lingua franca was a vehicular language made up of elements from various languages. It was used in restricted geographical areas for specific purposes and, hence, had no native speakers – think of Sabir, "the" lingua franca of the Mediterranean. Today, when we refer to a natural language, such as English or Chinese, as a lingua franca, we rather mean a national language often with hundreds of millions or, indeed, billions of native speakers (see, e.g., Dakhlia 2008; Ostler 2010). The contemporary meaning of "lingua franca" has hence retained the foreignness aspect in relation to its speakers; a lingua franca today is a foreign national language shared by speakers of other languages.

(2) Yet, the predominant contemporary notion of lingua franca has lost its connotations of political, cultural and ideological neutrality. When a (invariably widely spoken) national language attains the status of lingua franca in a region, it remains a language tied to particular states and their cultural and identity layers. Their use entails the need for teaching, teaching materials and exchange programmes, while also obviating the need for translation, interpreting and foreign language learning for native speakers of these languages. As noted in Chapter 2, lingua franca status accrues prestige and profits to the states in which the language

in question is the national language (and their citizens), and this alone precludes the possibility of neutrality.

Moreover, the question of the expressive value of language plays a pivotal part in the response to (2). This is not the place to revisit the acrimonious debate around whether natural languages have instrumental or expressive value. Suffice it to say that there is enough scientific consensus to support the notion that the languages we speak come to shape our identity layers and the way we view the world – to the same extent that we also come to shape these languages. Without subscribing to Herderian exceptionalism, to the Humboldt-Sapir-Whorf hypothesis (to quote George Steiner – see Leal 2019) or any kind of extreme linguistic relativism or determinism, it is still easy to see why such claims to the absolute neutrality of language and the instrumental or vehicular character of language (as made by ELF proponents) seems absurd. After all, can one consciously choose, among one's repertoire of languages, which one(s) will have an impact on one, and which one(s) will be used as mere instruments?

Incidentally, the reader will notice that Ó Riain does somewhat idealise the inner spirit of individual languages, particularly of the mother tongue. In contemporary linguistics, this terminological field has become a battlefield or a minefield – or perhaps both. In its more radically postmodern strains, the terminological debate goes as far as to deny the existence of languages as discrete units or bounded entities in the way that we have been referring to them in this book – "English," "Chinese," "French." The – very welcome and timely – intention is to call attention to the fact that languages are constructs, illusions put together artificially for purposes of nation building and warfare, as noted in Chapter 2. In this context, the notions of "mother tongue," "L1," "native speaker" and "foreign language" have also been duly deconstructed in the name of more fluidity and less emphasis both on languages as monolithic units and on language acquisition as a linear process (see, e.g., Pennycook 2006).

However, regardless of whether we perceive English as a national language or a lingua franca, a foreign language or a mother tongue, question (3) remains. Is there a need for a common language in the EU? This is yet another debate which would need a book of its own and which Ó Riain examines in detail in this chapter's interview. Traditionally, the need for a common language has been formulated as a prerequisite for the formation of a *demos*, of a public sphere in the Habermasian sense of *Öffentlichkeit* (Habermas 1962), as noted in Chapter 2. Remember the line in political theory, also mentioned in Chapter 2, which brings together thinkers such as John Stuart Mill, Karl Deutsch, Jürgen Habermas and Dieter Grimm around the need for a community of communication to be grounded in a common language for it to fulfil its democratic potential (see Leal 2021, 133–134). In fact, nearly all five of Robert Dahl's democracy criteria ("effective participation," "voting equality," "enlightened understanding," "control of the agenda," "inclusion of all adults") are predicated on a common language (Dahl 1988, 37–38 – see Leal 2021, 134).

Lying beneath these calls for unity around a shared language is sometimes the belief that language and identity go hand in hand. In fact, the quest for an EU identity, whatever that may be, has been at the forefront of the debate on the EU's fate and future since at least the 1990s, as noted in the previous chapters. Brexit has exacerbated some of the issues that arise in this discussion – had the British identified more with the EU, would they still have voted "leave" in the 2016 referendum? Will other EU member states follow suit if their levels of identification with the EU drop? As far as language policies, practices and ideologies are concerned, urgent research is needed to ascertain the extent to which the EU's use of English has alienated British voters and is possibly alienating voters in other member states – see Leal (2021, 197–198).

In this chapter's interview, Ó Riain speaks of a "NATO" kind of identity associated with the dominance of English in the EU. This, in his view, defeats the very objective of the EU as a "counterpoint" to the USA – culturally, politically, and ideologically. Due to its ineluctable ties, particularly to the USA, the English language, he claims, *cannot* strengthen a common European identity. Though this is not obvious from the interview, Ó Riain seems to echo a long list of thinkers who underline the traits that bring EU member states together, often in opposition to the USA – secularisation, the welfare state, the desire for an international order, along with faith in the state, the rule of law and human rights (Habermas & Derrida 2005, 9); "the Greek and Judeo-Christian heritage," "freedom and equality," "modern science," "the capitalistic form of production" and "justice achieved through class struggle" (Eco 2005, 15); "the gene of 'socialism'" (Vattimo 2005, 32); or, as Jean-Pierre Faye puts it, Europe is simply the place "where there is no death penalty" (quoted in Savater 2005, 43 – see Leal 2021, 136).

However homogenising and even excluding this list may sound (think of the importance of Islam in today's Europe, for instance), it does reflect what the EU wants to stipulate, descriptively but especially *normatively*, as its identity. Recent Eurobarometer surveys, for example, reveal that most citizens see democracy, the rule of law and human rights as the EU's main assets (Leal 2021, 136). The ongoing feud between the EU and Hungary (and to a certain extent, Poland) over the rule of law, along with the EU's efforts to tie the dispensing of funds to compliance with the rule of law, epitomises the debate around European identity.

To come back to the question of language, the view that English is associated with values incompatible with the EU hides immense complexity. We cannot untangle this completely here due to space constraints, but one thread is key for the purposes of the present book, namely that of identity. It is clear today that there is no easy formula connecting language to identity, as noted in Chapter 2. Much like "language," "identity" as a monolithic unit is an illusion – we ought to speak, rather, of *fluid identity layers* which we *perform* at all times. In this regard, language remains a *contingent* aspect of our identity layers, though one which is particularly pervasive, as it permeates virtually all other crucial factors, such as national, regional and local identification (see May 2004, 43–45; Blommaert 2006, 245–249; Pennycook 2006, 70).

To return to question (3), there does not seem to be a need for a lingua franca in the EU, as there is evidence that complex European public spheres, not unlike our complex identity layers, are emerging across language boundaries, as mentioned in Chapter 2. If anything, European identity – as a complex construct – seems predicated precisely on multilingualism and not on a yearning for a common language. This takes us back to a concern expressed by Ringe (2022, 198), namely that the EU's insistence on English as its lingua franca of sorts might exacerbate the current identity crisis, and that it will take more than a few symbolic, *de jure* nods to multilingualism to reverse that.

The European Commission and English as a "lingua franca" 69

I have suggested elsewhere (Leal 2021) that the EU needs a threefold turn as regards its language policies, practices and ideologies – a development that emerges in this chapter's interview. First, a language turn, to place language in the spotlight – not as a frill in the European project but as one of its pillars. Second, a translation turn, to make translations transparent and visible, to produce more translations into more languages and to attain a more equitable distribution of source and target languages. Third, a transcultural turn, to give intercomprehension a more prominent role in the bloc and gradually engender a more multilingual *modus operandi* in the EU. Each turn is accompanied by a set of concrete measures pertaining to the organisational aspects they entail (see Table 3.3).

Yet, as revealed in a recent interview, the current custodians of multilingualism in the EU, DGT, confirm that the trend is the opposite, at least in terms of translation. Less, not more, material is to be made available in languages other than English in the future, and more machine translation and freelancers should be employed at the expense of in-house translators (Leal 2021, 207–214). Ó Riain remains sceptical and critical of both developments – we will come back to these after the interview.

Interview

6 *How was your experience of multilingualism during your time at DGT, between September 2007 and August 2015, as seconded national expert for Ireland? How valued and present was multilingualism there? And how did you perceive the dominance of English in that context?*
A. When working in DGT, I was in charge of the Irish language section of the Commission's web translation unit, which had just been set up. It was probably one of the biggest units in the whole Commission, with more than 120 members, representing all 23 of the official languages – Croatia had not yet joined. There were between four and seven translators for each language – except Irish, for which I was given seven *stagiaires* or trainees, one after the other, to work under my direction, each of them for five months. They worked as translators into Irish, mainly from English but also from French and German. I had never been a translator, but I have a PhD in Irish and can write the language correctly.

Table 3.3 Three turns for the EU

	Awareness-raising measures	Organisational measures	Desirable official measures
Language turn	1. Awareness-raising campaigns (media and social media); 2. Summits on multilingualism (heads of state and/or government); 3. Awareness-raising talks, events and opinion polls (Commission representations in the member states)	4. Language delegations in all relevant EU subunits alternating in drafting the final version of documents and co-writing multilingual documents 5. Training in drafting multilingual texts 6. Training in intercomprehension and multilingual *modus operandi* 7. Recruitment of staff with more diverse language repertoires 8. Language goals in each subunit (e.g., equitable distribution of drafting languages, high number of languages represented in the department, large numbers of staff being trained in transcultural competence, intercomprehension and/or EU languages) 9. Salary increments to staff being trained in less widely spoken languages and in intercomprehension 10. Periodic statistics on language use and preferences in the EU available to the public	A. Language policy as shared competence B. Agency for language policy and planning C. Updated criteria for appointing official languages D. Increased budget for language services

	Awareness-raising measures	Organisational measures	Desirable official measures
Translation turn	11. Emphasis on the importance of translation/interpreting (measures 1–3) 12. Translations and originals visible by clear labelling	13. Multilingual training for translators 14. Expert multilingual groups in translation departments to compare translations across languages and ensure quality 15. More staff translators to increase output (including non-binding documents) 16. Periodic translation statistics available to the general public	
Transcultural turn	17. Emphasis on the importance of intercomprehension and transcultural competence (measures 1-3)	18. Courses on intercomprehension and transcultural competence in EU schools (alongside current language courses) 19. Subjects on multilingualism, migration and intercomprehension in teacher education 20. New, multilingual *modus operandi* grounded in multilingual communication and intercomprehension rather than in "lingua franca" communication	

Source: Leal (2021, 182–183).

My main function was to decide what needed to be translated into Irish, as DGT did not have the resources to translate everything. I was consulted all the time – there were two Swedish heads of unit, in succession, who did not speak any Irish, of course. They were both excellent heads of unit, who gave professional freedom to the translators. It was probably the least bureaucratic unit in the Commission. In the other parts of DGT, there was one assistant for every translator – the translators simply translated, and the assistants did everything to do with formatting, publishing etc. Whereas in the Web Translation Unit, there were only four assistants for over 120 translators, so most translators did all their own work and formatted and published their own texts, so it became a much more modern, much flatter structure. The Swedish Heads of Unit could not check their work. They had no inclination to second-guess translators and trusted their professionalism. They were fluent in English, French and Swedish.

Official multilingualism in theory became very monolingual in practice. The unit meetings were always in English only. If a French-speaking colleague said something in French, there was an objection right away from Eastern Europe, saying, "This is not allowed, you have to speak in English!" There was a Slovenian colleague who spoke very good Spanish and good German as well but didn't speak any French. She did not accept any international standing for French and objected to its use at unit meetings. This despite the fact that everybody else spoke French, and the majority language in Brussels is French. On occasion the Eastern Europeans even objected that the canteen staff could only speak French and demanded that only fluent English speakers should be employed! That objection got nowhere, of course, but it shows how any English-speaking EU institution in Brussels, Luxembourg or Strasbourg cuts itself off from its neighbouring European citizens.

I spent eight years there – I was originally seconded for two years, then got extensions until it became eight. A fascinating area – there are all kinds of things I could say about it. They set up an Irish language unit as well when I was there and appointed a head of unit who had no degree in Irish – which shows how contradictory these things can be. English was very dominant for all of the time I worked in DGT. The *DGT Info* always had articles in French as well as English. I wrote some articles in French as well as English for it. It was just those two languages – because not enough people understood German. Even among younger translators, probably about 60 per cent per cent had a good knowledge of German. To use German was therefore seen as excluding, whereas pretty much everybody had a good knowledge of English and French. As a spoken language there was a huge dominance of English.

The then Director General on one occasion replied to a French complaint that the proportion of documents drafted in French, which used to be the majority of documents before 1995, was now down to 14 per cent in that particular year (2010): "It's still too much. The proportion of native French speakers in the EU is 12 per cent per cent, so 14 per cent per cent is 2 per cent per cent too much." In other words, he saw English as *the* lingua franca, and saw its dominance as legitimate, but his reasoning applied to English only. He was a Swedish-speaking Finn who spoke fluent French and German, as well as Swedish and Finnish. However, he was very much against any particular position for French as an international language. This was his view, despite the fact that *La Francophonie* has 88 countries as members and observers, and French is by far the majority language in Brussels, spoken fluently by about 96 per cent of the people. I never understood his attitude. It shows that individual preferences can have a real influence if somebody is prepared to use their position to further their own preferences. It can tell the other way around as well: the President of the Commission, Ursula von der Leyen – one of the reasons she received strong French support is that she is a fluent French speaker.

7 The use of English as a drafting language rose from 45.4 per cent in 1997 to 62 per cent in 2007, 72.5 per cent in 2008 and then 85.5 per cent in 2020. The percentage of EU law originally drafted in English is estimated at 95 per cent, and a 2009 survey of staff in the European Commission found that 90 per cent used English as their main drafting language, whereas 95 per cent considered English the most used language in performing their duties in 2016. Though legally binding documents are available in all 24 official languages, non-binding texts are increasingly drafted in English and not translated at all. Yet legally, all 24 EU languages class as official and working languages. How do you perceive this trend towards English as an unofficial lingua franca of sorts? Is it a good candidate to play this role – and does the EU need a lingua franca at all?

A. The constant increase in the proportion of documents drafted in English alone and the lack of drafting in other languages is a fact. I see that development rather negatively because I saw what can happen in practice: texts being drafted in English by native speakers of French, in sub-optimal English, and then being translated back into French by a translator. It would have been so much easier for the competent French-speaking official to draft directly in French. There was this feeling that English is *the* European lingua franca, therefore all are obliged to draft in English. I have seen meetings in the Commission where you had 20 fluent speakers of French all discussing fluently in French, then *one* Eastern European arrives who does not speak French, and suddenly everybody, all 21, had to switch to English. Their English was reasonably good for most of the 20, but only reasonably good, not very good. That meant that the standard of discussion, and of drafting, drops, and drops quite a lot, because people are no longer allowed to use their first language, which they know so much better than any other language. There is a real difference – a well-educated native speaker tends to know their own language better than almost any learner can. Imagine the difficulty of somebody from outside Poland learning Polish and then writing Polish as well as those who grew up and lived all their lives in Poland. The same is true of all languages.

The practice of drafting in English clearly led to a decline in the quality of drafting. Occasionally the translators phoned the original writer. A French translator would phone a French official and say, "*Qu'est-ce que vous voulez dire avec ce mot, cette phrase? Ça ne se dit pas comme ça en anglais. Dites-le-moi en français parce que c'est plus facile.*" The good thing is that translators did have a habit of phoning the author, to discover what precisely he or she meant. I think it was far better when people could draft in their own language. Clearly you cannot have people drafting in all 24 languages, as very few could check what they've written, but drafting only in English causes a sharp decline in quality.

I remember the figures when I worked at the Commission in Brussels. Counting all categories of staff, a large majority of certainly were fluent French speakers – they were either Belgian or from France, Luxembourg or some other French-speaking country. Deciding that these colleagues are not allowed to draft in French appears to be based on an ideology that English is *the* lingua franca, therefore people *must* "choose" English. The overall quality of work is suffering because of this English-only ideology, as Professor Robert Phillipson pointed out in his 2003 book, *English-Only Europe?*. My wife is French and worked for many years at the EU institutions. Again and again, she saw examples of people drafting very well in French being told, "Sorry, your superior two grades above doesn't read French, so you have to draft in English." It meant that drafting was then done in English and very poorly. Again, language can have political importance on occasion, but at the same time there was a contradictory feeling that language is not important at all. English is just a neutral code and has nothing to do with British and American culture. That supposition is demonstrably mistaken, as I saw again and again while working in the Commission.

Can English really ever be a neutral instrument? Can ELF [English as a lingua franca], or "Euro-English," be a separate English from the English spoken by native speakers? Many years of diplomatic experience have convinced me that they cannot. Native speakers set the norm in every language. During 44 years of diplomatic service, on countless occasions I witnessed colleagues deferring to UK and Irish colleagues to check what was "correct"; not once did I witness a UK or Irish colleagues deferring to any ELF or Euro-English putative norm. This clearly gives native English speakers undue influence on policy formation.

The only exception to native speaker dominance that I can recall is the Normans in England. There were some sounds in English which they could not pronounce: for instance, the "gh" in words like "night" became silent, and was no longer pronounced as in Old English, where it had been similar to a voiced "ch" [as in Scottish "loch"]. Due to Norman political, economic and military dominance, the native speakers started to follow the Norman pronunciation. This is exceedingly rare; native speakers do not copy learners but tend to laugh at their mistakes, and learners tend to be very sensitive to the views of native speakers. Admittedly, there are more second language speakers than native speakers of English. This fact, which may appear important to theoreticians, is entirely irrelevant in practice, in my experience.

Every language tends to have its own internal spirit, and English is no exception. English is associated with a free market, liberal, economic spirit. Some in France and other countries are critical of the Commission for having taken not only the English language but also the Anglo-Saxon approach to economics as well. They see this as lightening regulation, so that the stronger do well, and the weaker less well.

[This is the theory behind this no-policy language policy as well. In my interviews with the current heads of DGT, they say the same thing. They say, "Well, everybody happens to speak English anyway, it is the most spoken language in Europe, so we haven't really taken a decision to promote it," but in fact they have. There's no "we just sort of go with the flow, the market decides which language has the most value and we just follow." If you're an international or, in this case, a supranational organisation, your decisions impact an entire continent and the whole world. You don't just go with the flow; you have to take a stand. There is a German political theorist [Peter A. Kraus] who says that the European Union promoting English is a bit like giving Microsoft a subsidy to produce software.]

An excellent analogy. The widespread use of English has both advantages and disadvantages. Everybody sees the advantages, but few appear to see the disadvantages. I think one disadvantage of English in the EU is that it is weakening European identity. English is very much a world language, with the largest concentration of its native speakers being in the United States. Therefore, the use of English in Europe tends to strengthen a kind of NATO identity, with the United States as the centre. It actually militates against the development of any specifically European identity. There are 336 million people living in the United States, and the large majority will be native English speakers. There is no language in Europe with this number of native speakers. Euro-Atlantic integration, due to the dominance of English, is often confused with European integration, though the two are very different. The idea of a European Europe, an independent Europe, is weakened by the use of English as the only common language. My Esperanto-speaking friends sometimes joke about NATO, referring to it "North American Talk Only!"

[I think you're quite clear on this part about whether you think English is a good candidate to play the role of the lingua franca of the EU. But the question is: does the EU need a lingua franca, do you think there should be a formal decision taken, you know, "This is our lingua franca." Is this necessary?]

I think a lingua franca is useful in the sense that the right lingua franca can strengthen European unity, in harmony with its diversity, on condition that multilingualism remains a strong pillar of European integration. Things like song – my children learned the Latin version of the European anthem in the European School in Brussels, and they learned the Esperanto version from me.

[So you see this role for a potential lingua franca more at the symbolic level – for example, the anthem. Or do you think there should be a language – as you were saying earlier – when you have meetings or when you draft documents, one should give preference to just one language?]

Ideally, if I had a magic wand and I could just change things as I wished, I would have all the Council of Ministers and all the members of European Parliament speaking in their own languages, so that they say precisely what they want to say rather than what they are able to say. This would markedly improve the quality of contributions and, in addition, all the languages would be heard regularly, with interpreters interpreting only into a neutral language like Esperanto, so that everyone would be expected to understand the European lingua franca. This would actually allow us to expand the number of EU official working languages – you could add all the languages excluded at present, such as Catalan, Basque, Galician, Breton, Mirandés –, including the more widely-used immigrant languages such as Arabic, Turkish and others. Instead of just 24 official languages, the EU could have 40 or more, and the overall costs of this wider multilingualism would be drastically reduced. Professional multilingual interpreters would only need a few months of training. Those who understand any Romance language already have 90 per cent of the vocabulary of Esperanto. So, we would have linguistic diversity – far more diversity than at present and not just three or four languages.

From a legal point of view, EU agreement on one language to be the original language for all legal texts would represent huge progress. It would provide a legal certainty that simply cannot exist when you have versions of documents in many languages, and all of them with equal legal validity. English is particularly poorly placed to be this language, as Britain's Common Law system is very unlike the legal system of Continental countries. This is why French remains the language of discussion at the European Court of Justice, and why all judgments are initially promulgated in

French, before being translated into the other official languages. This situation inevitably advantages native speakers of French. It is tolerated, as the dominance of English in the other EU institutions puts non-native speakers of English at a disadvantage. Agreement for EU texts on a neutral language such as Esperanto would be a huge step forward, as it would advantage nobody, would enhance legal certainty and would end linguistic disputes concerning the precise meaning of legal texts. It would make non-discrimination a fact, rather than a pious aspiration, and this may influence other parts of the world.

An EU lingua franca could be useful if it were a true lingua franca, i.e., not the language of any country. It would prevent schoolchildren drawing the unfortunate conclusion that "my language was chosen as the EU lingua franca; it is therefore better than your language, and I am better than you." Esperanto is like a "linguistic handshake," where each person extends their hand halfway, meeting the other in friendship as an equal.

[You make a clear point that Esperanto is about opening a door towards multilingualism; it's not, as you say, an end in itself.]

As a supporter of multilingualism, I would, of course, oppose Esperanto as the sole language, but I favour Esperanto as a learning tool because I think it really does help. My own two daughters, with whom I speak only Irish, learned Esperanto as a fifth language. My wife, who spoke Esperanto fairly well, was against it as a fifth language because she felt that the four languages our children already spoke were enough. I got some children's books from China in Esperanto, read them aloud to the children, and they had only one new word per page. Because they spoke French, English and German, they could already follow the stories, without ever having studied Esperanto. So, my wife agreed, and then four summers in a row we sent them to Esperanto summer camps. The first was in Italy. There were about 50 children from 20 countries whose only common language was Esperanto. They had one week in Italy, and a week in each of the following three years. In those four weeks, they picked up Esperanto. They never had formal classes, but just played with children who spoke the language, and subsequent experience showed me that they had mastered it.

One further example: Helmar Frank, professor of cybernetics at Paderborn University, Germany, was offered a semester in Brazil to teach a cybernetics course. He spoke German and English, but not Portuguese. He was a fluent Esperanto speaker, however, and he organised an intensive weekend course in Esperanto for his Brazilian students. This was all they needed. He was then able to deliver his lectures in Esperanto and the students could follow him. One weekend's study would not have been enough for French, English or any other language, but it was enough for Esperanto, for speakers of a Romance language like Portuguese.

8 *In my recent book, I recommend three turns to engender a multilingual* modus operandi *in the EU, namely a language turn, a translation turn and a transcultural turn. In a nutshell, the language turn entails a new awareness of the role of multilingualism in the bloc, not as a frill in the European project but rather as a key element of our identity repertoires. The translation turn calls for more translations to be made available into more languages, and for translation and interpreting to be made visible. The transcultural turn encompasses measures to foster intercomprehension and transcultural skills both in Brussels and in the member states (through the education systems, which are currently geared towards English). These measures, albeit admittedly idealistic, would place language and translation in the spotlight and transform the bloc into a more multilingual union, truly united in diversity. How can these measures be complemented and/or adapted to achieve the desired results?*

A. I would strongly agree with the need to place language and translation in the spotlight and increase awareness of their importance. There is a general feeling in the EU institutions, indeed in society in general, that language is just a tool, a neutral tool that has no particular importance. In my view, this idea is fundamentally mistaken. Language creates identity. It is an expression of the culture and history of a people. There is so much which cannot be easily expressed in other languages. Machine translation, for instance, can sometimes produce acceptable text, and give a general idea of the original. It is not a precision instrument and can get things completely wrong. To cite some rather amusing examples: The expression, "the spirit is willing, but the flesh is weak," was machine-translated into Russian, and produced "the whiskey is good, but the meat is undercooked!" The phrase "out of sight, out of mind" was machine-translated into Russian as "invisible lunatic." A final example narrowly avoided tragedy: the Russian word "*мир*" (mir) means both "peace" and "the world."

At US–Soviet negotiations during the Cold War, the Russian side said, "We demand peace (*'мир'*)," but a machine mistranslated this as "we demand the world!"

Having worked with DGT and having worked with languages for many years, I can see that language is a minefield, that you need a human being who understands the cultural background of a text. I heard the phrase on one occasion in DGT, "You don't need to understand this, just translate it," as if translation were some kind of mechanical process. This shows a deep lack of awareness of the importance of language, and indeed, of how language functions.

Frequently, at EU coordination meetings here in Vienna for the last five years, colleagues say, "I have a point to make, but it's just a linguistic point," which has the idea that it is not a substantive point. A linguistic point can be very substantive indeed. We need only mention the famous UN Security Council Resolution 242, at the end of the Six-Day War in 1967, where the presence or absence of the definite article makes all the difference. The English text of Resolution 242, accepted by the US and Israel, does not have the definite article, and called for Israeli withdrawal "from territories occupied," leaving the question of the territories from which Israel should withdraw to be negotiated. The French version calls for Israeli withdrawal "*des territoires occupés,*" i.e., the use of the definite article makes clear that the withdrawal is to be from all the territories occupied during the Six-Day War, including east Jerusalem. The US made clear that it would have used its veto right to block this French interpretation, and that it accepted only the English version of Resolution 242.

The present dominance of English clearly gives an advantage to native speakers in drafting texts. Despite the questioning of the concept of the "native speaker" in linguistics, no such questioning exists in the field of diplomacy, in my experience. The English speaker who may not like one particular political viewpoint can always say, "That doesn't sound well in English, so we need to say it in a different way," and he/she says it in a way which fundamentally alters the meaning, precisely as he/she wishes. Other colleagues tend to acquiesce: "You're the native English speaker, whatever you think sounds well, we will accept." I have seen this happen again and again: the massive advantage of native speakers. It is really important to value languages, to have people using their own language, their mother tongue, more and more because they can say exactly what they want to say. If they are using English, they say what they are able to say, not what they want to say. Again, I have seen this with texts in the Commission being produced by non-native speakers in English and not being well produced. There were always questions as to what exactly they meant.

Intercomprehension is very important, and its importance is all too often ignored. Languages like Spanish, French and Italian have so much in common, particularly if a person speaks slowly and clearly. I remember once seeing a recording of a Russian who was in Serbia speaking in English to colleagues, and then he used a phrase in Russian, which the Serbs understood instantaneously. The Serb said, "Our languages are so related, why are we using English?" Serbian and Russian are quite close, two Slavic languages, they have a lot in common. English is much more distant from both. If we had classes in school on intercomprehension, more people could speak in their mother tongue and be understood by far more people – instead of resorting to poorly learned English, with all of the ambiguities inherent to that language.

Following years of experience in this area, I would say that most learners of English, though they learn it very well, almost never reach native speaker level. Perhaps one in every 100,000 does. This is true of every ethnic language. The native speaker has spent a lifetime mastering so many layers of language, and so many different registers, that are impossible for a learner to emulate. For instance, although I have spoken French daily for most of my life, I would not expect to win in a French language competition against a native French speaker. I developed in Irish and English but not in French. I do not have French reactions or French cultural referents. Actors or singers who are household names in France will be unfamiliar to me, and it will always be like this. I speak German fluently, have had two postings in Austria, for eight years, and have lived in Berlin for four years. I use German comfortably, but that does not make me a native speaker of German.

One of the strongest arguments in favour of a role for a neutral language like Esperanto is precisely this: that it gives an equality and an equal opportunity in communication that does not exist otherwise, and it would bring languages and language policy centre stage in a way that the use of English never can. Teaching intercomprehension would also help enormously, but it does not help between speakers of different language families, e.g., between speakers of Romance and Slavic languages. This is where I see a role for Esperanto, which is about 10 times easier to learn than any other language. It was initiated in Poland, so it does have some Slavic elements, for instance penultimate syllable stress, as in Polish. Over 99.2 per cent of the language is taken from other languages with minimal change to the original, but it is no more a mixture of languages than English is a mixture of German and French. Esperanto may appear superficially similar to western European languages, but at a deeper level, it has a grammatical system not shared by any Indo-European language.

Zamenhof saw initiating this language as his life's work. Being Jewish, he had a very good knowledge of Biblical Hebrew, and thus knew a non-Indo-European language thoroughly. His language superficially appears to be a mixture of Indo-European languages, but the deeper you go into it, the more non-European it becomes. At the second level, it's more an agglutinative language, like Turkish or Hungarian, as seen in, for instance, "hospital" = *"malsanulejo,"* composed of *"mal+san+ul+ejo."* The basic root is *"sana,"* meaning "healthy," *"mal"* is the opposite of healthy, so "ill," *"ul"* means a person and *"ejo"* means a place, so "place for persons not in health." Apparently, the Chinese version is quite close to this. Therefore, a Chinese person learning Esperanto will need to learn these European roots, but then they produce more complex expressions or words, as in Chinese. At the deepest level, Esperanto is an isolating language like Mandarin Chinese or Vietnamese, it is composed of invariable morphemes, which can either combine to make compound words, or each of which can function as independent words.

In English you have different morphemes for the same unit of meaning, such as "see," "sight," "visibility." You do not have that in Esperanto – you have one morpheme, *"vid,"* which expresses the idea of seeing. Then, *"mi vidas"* is "I see," *"vido"* is *"a sight,"* *"nevidebla"* is "invisible," *"videbleco"* is *"visibility."* The basic morpheme is the invariable *"vid,"* which is similar to Mandarin Chinese, but where Chinese and Esperanto really resemble each other is when each of the elements in a word can become an independent word. The morpheme *"mal"* means the opposite, and so *"male"* means "on the contrary," turning it into an adverb. *"Sana"* is "healthy," *"sanigi"* is "to make somebody or something healthy." The *"ig"* came from Hebrew, originally, and it can turn every adjective, without exception, into a verb, but this device does not exist in any Indo-European language. For example, "*sana*" to "*sanigi,*" "*pura*" to "*purigi*" – "*pura*" is "clean" and "*purigi*" "to clean." One further example: the suffix "*-il*" means an "instrument." Added to any verb it gives the word for "the instrument to carry out the function of that verb." Thus "*kudrilo,*" from "*kudri + ilo,*" is "a sewing needle;" "*skribilo*" is "a pen," "*ludilo*" is a toy, "*trancilo*" is a knife, etc.

When a role for a neutral language is proposed, the most frequent argument used against it is that "it has no culture." But one of the foremost specialists in this area, Professor Detlev Blanke of the Humboldt University Berlin, defended the position that culture resides in the people who use a language, not in the actual words. Taking the word "*famille*" in French, or "family" in English: by what logic can it be said that these two words have culture and "*familio,*" in Esperanto, does not? All three have the same Latin origin, "*familia,*" and about 99.2 per cent of the vocabulary of Esperanto is similar to this. The Esperanto word "*episkopo*" is actually closer to the original Ancient Greek word "*episkopos*" than the Italian "*vescovo,*" the Spanish "*obispo,*" the Portuguese "*bispo,*" the French "*évêque,*" the English "bishop," the German "*Bischof*" or the Irish "*easpag.*" The linguist Mario Pei once said that to call modern Esperanto "an artificial language" is like "calling an automobile an artificial horse."

Esperanto's vocabulary has the same origins as these European languages, plus the non-European syntax, which is strange in some ways because Zamenhof did not speak Mandarin Chinese. He knew Biblical Hebrew well enough to translate the whole Old Testament from Hebrew into Esperanto. He also knew Ancient Greek, Latin, Polish, Russian, German and French extremely well, and learned enough English to translate Shakespeare's *Hamlet* into Esperanto. He studied to become a doctor at Moscow University and became an eye specialist in Vienna. His idea was that Esperanto should contain the most useful features of all the languages he knew. As a young boy, Zamenhof witnessed quarrels in the streets in Białystok, due to misunderstandings. There were five languages in use in a city of some 30,000 people: Polish, German, Russian, Belarussian and Yiddish. He was part of the Jewish majority, who were at the bottom of the social scale. The Russians had political power; commercial life was dominated by Germans, but the

Yiddish of the Jews had little or no prestige. However, Zamenhof wrote poetry in Yiddish, and respected its traditions.

Ideally schools should respect all the languages of multilingual children. If somebody speaks Turkish or Arabic, that is a valuable resource. All languages give access to a distinctive culture and way of thinking that is not present in other languages. The monolingual mindset, "one country, one language," and the idea that language can be a neutral tool, are mistaken, even though they are widespread among decision-makers. While it is, of course, true that the economy is extremely important, it would be a mistake to believe that it is the only important thing. That is the mistake that the European institutions have made, particularly over the past 15 years or so. It is not the fault of any one individual – it is a systemic fault. People accept this belief that languages are not important, therefore multilingualism is a waste of time, and English is a neutral instrument. English is a product of English and American culture and history. It is rooted in a very old and a very rich tradition and can never be a neutral instrument.

I value English, I grew up in an English-speaking part of Ireland. I see English as a red rose, a very beautiful and popular flower. However, how many of us would like a garden full of red roses, which has no other flower? This is precisely the danger with the present worldwide system of the unquestioned dominance of English, and this idea that it is just a neutral instrument to be learned, like mathematics. That is as wrong as the accepted wisdom 150 years ago that human beings would never fly because any machine that they construct would be heavier than air. Until people actually saw aeroplanes flying, they still believed that it was impossible. In a future, more enlightened, time when people understand the importance of languages better, they may look back at our present age as a rather primitive stage of humanity. This theme is dealt with brilliantly in William Auld's original poem in Esperanto, "*La infana raso*" (The Infant Race), which has been translated into over 10 languages.

Commentary

Ó Riain's appraisal of multilingualism in the EU – particularly in DGT – shows Van Parijs's "maxi-min principle" in action – see Chapter 2. Several key questions emerge here regarding the practical value of multilingualism, the abyss between language policy and practice, as well as the appetite to go into these questions in the EU – or lack thereof. To single out one crucial point mentioned by Ó Riain, research shows that that "EU actors use English at a seventh-grade reading level on average, compared to the eleventh-grade reading level used by native English lawmakers elsewhere" (Ringe 2022, 143 – see also 154). In other words, the maxi-min principle pulls the quality of EU political debate down significantly; yet it seems that the predominant language ideologies compel most to settle on a common language (today English) at any cost.

More research is needed to ascertain why this is the case. One could speculate that the "one nation, one language" mentality at the heart of the (both top-down *and* bottom-up) process of nation building in Europe has led to a tacit agreement on the need for monolingualism – or, in other words, a certain "intolerance" of multilingual conversations based on intercomprehension. This scenario is somewhat different in countries like Brazil which, despite having had its linguistic landscape flattened almost completely by colonialism,[2] are more open to passive multilingualism; and completely different in countries such as South Africa, in which multilingual conversations are everyday occurrences (see Leal 2012).

The three turns I propose and the changes that Ó Riain envisages for the EU are predicated on a shift in this mentality in Europe. Whereas the threefold turn for the EU (see Table 3.3) attempts to bridge the gap between the EU's language policies and practices, Ó Riain's vision entails a significant expansion of the EU's institutional linguistic landscape. The introduction of Esperanto as a *de jure* and *de facto* lingua franca would allow for the expansion of the EU's language repertoire, so his argument goes, encompassing migrant languages as well.

If we recall the definition of lingua franca presented earlier, Esperanto is undoubtedly a better suited candidate than any national language. After all, it is not the national language of any country, nor does it accrue profits and prestige to its native speakers – though it is estimated that there are about 1,000 of them in different countries. Ironically, as noted in Chapter 2, this lack of geopolitical boundedness is its Achilles' heel. Indeed, many perceive Esperanto as an *artificial* language *deprived of culture* – two common misconceptions, as noted by Ó Riain. More importantly,

Table 3.4 Esperanto grammar

Pronunciation
Written as pronounced, no exceptions. 1 letter = 1 sound (28 letters). Stress always on penultimate syllable.
c: /ts/   ĉ: /ch/   j: /y/   ĝ: /j/   ŝ: /sh/   ŭ: /w/

Grammar
The final letter indicates the part of speech.

Noun	adjective	adverb	plural	direct object
o	a	e	j	n

Ŝi trinkas kafon kaj skribas interesajn librojn energie kaj saĝe.
She drinks coffee and writes interesting books energetically and wisely.

Verbs
Verb endings indicate tense and mood – no irregular verbs.

i	as	is	os	us	u
INFINITIVE	PRESENT	PAST	FUTURE	CONDITIONAL	IMPERATIVE
helpi	mi helpas	vi helpis	li helpos	ŝi helpus	ni helpu! helpu!
to help	I help	you helped	he will help	she would help	let's help! help!

Vocabulary
40 prefixes and suffixes reduce vocabulary learning to a minimum.
For example,
varma = warm, varmega = hot, varmeta = lukewarm, malvarma = cold, varmigi = to heat
bovo = an ox, bovino = a cow, bovido = a calf, virbovo = a bull

Examples
Saluton, kiel vi? = Hi, how are you?
Bone, dankon. Kiel vi nomiĝas? = I'm well, thanks. What's your name?
Mi nomiĝas Ana, kaj vi? Kion vi faras? = My name is Ana, and you? What do you do?
Mia nomo estas Adam, mi estas studento. = I'm Adam, I'm a student.
Ho, bonege! Venu, ni trinku ion! = Oh, great! Come on, let's have something to drink!

Source: Adapted from esperanto-france.org (see also esperanto12.net – both links last accessed in January 2023).

however, not being a national language entails a lack of political backing which, when it comes to language, is crucial.

Research shows that Esperanto is significantly easier to learn, particularly for speakers of languages in the Germanic, Romance and Slavic families – Table 3.4 offers an overview of the language. Esperanto does enjoy some backing in academic circles and has been endorsed, in different disciplines, as a viable element to contribute to multilingualism (see, e.g., Bormann 1970; Phillipson 2003; Grin 2008, 2011; Fiedler & Brosch 2018). Normatively, Esperanto constitutes the only reasonable, just, alternative – perhaps alongside the more elitist Latin – if one wanted to go down the lingua franca route. Ó Riain's vision of increased multilingualism enabled by Esperanto as bridge language is a theoretically sound "bridge" in the sense of both accelerating language learning and pairing up with other languages in translation and interpreting. Yet the current linguistic landscape is dominated by the "one nation, one language" mentality plus English, which is gaining (yet more) ground in the EU's education systems (see, e.g., European Commission/EACEA/Eurydice 2017). A shift towards Esperanto, however desirable both normatively and in practical terms, seems unlikely in the foreseeable future.

If a gradual shift in mentality were to take place – as a response both to top-down and bottom-up measures and grassroots initiatives, including those in Table 3.3 – it seems more likely that a wider acceptance and use of intercomprehension would precede any increased openness to Esperanto. This is due not only to the ideological factors mentioned earlier, but also because of practical constraints, such as the lack of university departments and degrees devoted to Esperanto and the concomitant lack of trained translators and interpreters. However, as Ó Riain and many others reiterate (see, e.g., Fielder & Brosch 2018), introducing Esperanto as a subject, say, in school or university, does not require nearly as much time or as many resources as introducing a national language, so ultimately the main barriers are ideological.

In this chapter's interview, Ó Riain expresses a concern over the feasibility of a more multilingual *modus operandi* for the EU – for example, regarding multilingual drafting – suggesting, instead, an increase in the number of source languages and a reduction of target languages to one, i.e., Esperanto. This concern over the viability of an increased role for intercomprehension and multilingual drafting and negotiating was echoed throughout the interviews I conducted in different EU institutions, bodies and agencies in 2020 (see Leal 2021). The opinion of DGT in this area epitomises this concern, as they categorically state that "multi-drafting [multilingual drafting] is unrealistic" and that "drafting happens in a language that allows all those concerned to contribute" – i.e., today English (Leal 2021, 209, 213). Interestingly, in 2012, DGT themselves published the results of a study on the potential impact of intercomprehension on their own workings, concluding that intercomprehension would allow for the establishment of a "multilingual concordance" group to compare translations across all 24 languages, an "external translation" group to assess the quality of translations done by freelancers, as well as a "training" group to grant other translators, particularly in the departments of French and English, access to other languages in their language families (European Commission 2012 – see Leal 2021, 165).

As we advance into the second half of this book, we will return to the main consequences of the EU's current linguistic regime, as well as to alternatives to its *modus operandi*. Some of the key issues include the prestige native speakers of English automatically enjoy and the concomitant control of the agenda, the linguistic injustices entailed in the pecking order among EU languages, the current *laissez-faire* or no-policy language policy mentality that dominates EU policy-making in the realm of language, the soft – and often overlooked – power of language and the EU's utilitarian, mechanistic notion of translation.

Notes

1 Braj Kachru's (1985) much-quoted image of the three concentric circles in the spread of English worldwide has become a staple in any discussion of the role of Shakespeare's language today. The inner circle consists of "norm-providing" countries where English is spoken as a first language, typically in Great Britain and Ireland, North America, Australia and New Zealand. Some include many more countries and territories in this list, such as Jamaica and Trinidad and Tobago (Ostler 2010, 33). Immediately after the inner circle comes the outer circle with "norm-developing" countries, i.e., places where English has been institutionalised as one of the official languages, as is the case in most former British colonies. The third and outermost circle is the expanding

circle of "norm-dependent" countries, i.e., places where English enjoys no special status and is thus a foreign language, such as most of the EU or Brazil. We have to imagine these circles as ripples in a pond, overlapping and in constant motion (McArthur, cited in Kachru 2005, 13 – see also Leal 2021, 26).

2 According to Daniel Munduruku, one of Brazil's main voices in the literature by original nations, there are about 275 indigenous languages spoken in the country's territory today, most of which are entirely undocumented and only beginning to be studied now (private communication).

References

Barbier, Jean-Claude. 2018. "European integration and the variety of languages: An awkward co-existence." In *The politics of multilingualism: Europeanisation, globalisation and linguistic governance*, edited by François Grin and Peter A. Kraus, 333–357. Amsterdam & Philadelphia: John Benjamins.

Bengoetxea, Joxerramon. 2011. "Multilingual and multicultural legal reasoning: The European Court of Justice." In *Linguistic diversity and European democracy*, edited by Anne Lise Kjaer and Silvia Adamo, 97–122. Farnham: Ashgate.

Blommaert, Jan. 2006. "Language policy and national identity." In *An introduction to language policy: Theory and method*, edited by Thomas Ricento, 238–254. Oxford: Blackwell Publishing.

Bormann, Werner. 1970. "Sprachenproblem in den europäischen Institutionen." *La monda lingvo-problemo* 2: 114–126.

Dahl, Robert A. 1988. *On democracy*. New Haven: Yale University Press.

Dakhlia, Jocelyne. 2008. *Lingua franca: Histoire d'une langue métisse en Méditerranée*. Paris: Actes Sud.

Eco, Umberto. 2005. "An uncertain Europe between rebirth and decline." In *Old Europe, new Europe, core Europe: Transatlantic relations after the Iraq War*, edited by Daniel Levy, Max Pensky and John Torpey, 14–20. London & New York: Verso.

European Commission. 2009. *Translating for a multilingual community*. Luxembourg: Office for Official Publications of the European Communities.

European Commission. 2012. *Studies on translation and multilingualism: Intercomprehension*. Luxembourg: Publications Office of the European Union.

European Commission/EACEA/Eurydice. 2017. *Key data on teaching languages at school in Europe: Eurydice report*. Luxembourg: Publications Office of the European Union.

European Parliament. n.d. *Which languages are in use in the Parliament?* www.europarl.europa.eu/news/en/faq/21/which-languages-are-in-use-in-the-parliament.

Fiedler, Sabine, and Cyril Brosch. 2018. "Should a planned language such as Esperanto be promoted as an international lingua franca?" In *Mobility and inclusion in multilingual Europe: The MIME Vademecum*, edited by François Grin, 150–151.

Gardner, Jeremy. 2016. *Misused English words and expressions in EU publications*. European Court of Auditors.

Grin, François. 2008. "Principles of policy evaluation and their application to multilingualism in the European Union." In *Respecting linguistic diversity in the European Union*, edited by Xabier Arzoz, 73–83. Amsterdam & Philadelphia: John Benjamins.

Grin, François, interview by European Commission. 2011. *Lingua franca: Chimera or reality?* 59–70.

Habermas, Jürgen. 1962. *Strukturwandel der Öffentlichkeit. Untersuchungen zu einer Kategorie der bürgerlichen Gesellschaft*. Darmstadt & Neuwied: Luchterhand Verlag.

Habermas, Jürgen, and Jacques Derrida. 2005. "February 15, or, what binds us together: Plea for a common foreign policy, beginning in core Europe." In *Old Europe, new Europe, core Europe: Transatlantic relations after the Iraq War*, edited by Daniel Levy, Max Pensky and John Torpey, translated by Max Pensky, 3–13. London & New York: Verso.

Jenkins, Jennifer. 2007. *English as a lingua franca: Attitude and identity*. Oxford: Oxford: Oxford University Press.

Jenkins, Jennifer, and Alessia Cogo. 2010. "English as a lingua franca in Europe: A mismatch between policy and practice." *European journal of language policy* 2 (2): 271–294.

Kachru, Braj B. 1985. "Standards, codification and sociolinguistic realism: The English language in the outer circle." In *English in the world: Teaching and learning the language and literatures*, edited by Randolph Quirk and Henry G. Widdowson, 11–30. Cambridge: Cambridge University Press.

Kachru, Braj B. 2005. *Asian Englishes: Beyond the canon*. Hong Kong: Hong Kong University Press.

Kachru, Braj B., Yamuna Kachru, and Cecil L. Nelson (ed.). 2006. *The handbook of World Englishes*. Malden: Blackwell Publishing.

Leal, Alice. 2012. "Mehrsprachigkeit: Brasilien, Österreich und die Europäische Union." In *Die Multiminoritätengesellschaft*, edited by Mary Snell-Hornby and Mira Kadrić, 45–53. Berlin: SAXA Verlag.

Leal, Alice. 2019. "Equivalence." In *The Routledge handbook of translation and philosophy*, edited by Piers Rawling and Philip Wilson, 224–242. Abingdon & New York: Routledge.

Leal, Alice. 2021. *English and translation in the European Union: Unity and multiplicity in the wake of Brexit*. Abingdon & New York: Routledge.

May, Stephen. 2004. "Rethinking linguistic human rights: Answering questions of identity, essentialism and mobility." In *Language rights and language survival*, edited by Jane Freeland and Donna Patrick, 35–53. Manchester: St. Jerome Publishing.

Modiano, Marko. 2009. "Inclusive/exclusive? English as a lingua franca in the European Union." *World Englishes* 28 (2): 208–223.

Modiano, Marko. 2017. "English in a post-Brexit European Union." *World Englishes* 36 (3): 313–327.

Ostler, Nicholas. 2010. *The last lingua franca: The rise and fall of world languages*. London: Penquin Books.

Pennycook, Alastair. 2006. "Postmodernism in language policy." In *An introduction to language policy: Theory and method*, edited by Thomas Ricento, 60–76. Malden: Blackwell Publishing.

Phillipson, Robert. 2003. *English-only Europe?: Challenging language policy*. London & New York: Routledge.

Ringe, Nils. 2022. *The Language(s) of politics: Multilingual policy-making in the European Union*. Michigan: The University of Michigan Press.

Robinson, William. 2014. "Translating legislation: The European Union." *The Theory and Practice of Legislation* 2 (2): 185–210.

Savater, Fernando. 2005. "Europe, both needed and in need." In *Old Europe, new Europe, core Europe: Transatlantic relations after the Iraq war*, edited by Daniel Levy, Max Pensky and John Torpey, 41–43. London & New York: Verso.

Seidlhofer, Barbara. 2011. *Understanding English as a lingua franca*. Oxford: Oxford University Press.

Van Parijs, Philippe. 2011. *Linguistic justice for Europe and for the world*. Oxford: Oxford University Press.

Vattimo, Gianni. 2005. "The European Union faces the major points of its development." In *Old Europe, new Europe, core Europe: Transatlantic relations after the Iraq war*, edited by Daniel Levy, Max Pensky and John Torpey, 28–33. London & New York: Verso.

Wright, Sue. 2007. "English in the European Parliament: MEPs and their language repertoires." *SOCIOLINGUISTICA* 21: 151–165.

4 Migrant and non-territorial languages in the EU

Introductory remarks

The discussion on the European Charter for Regional or Minority Languages (ECRML), in Chapter 1, helped to map the EU's linguistic landscape beyond its 24 official languages. This chapter will zoom in on the EU's migrant and non-territorial languages, while also taking stock of the bloc's overall language hierarchies. The interview with Ó Riain includes an appraisal of the importance of migrant and non-territorial languages in the EU; suggestions of possible frameworks in which to embed these languages; the introduction of the notion of "parity of esteem" in relation to language; as well as the suggestion of a role for a neutral language to facilitate the integration of immigrants in their host societies.

Roughly 200 languages are considered indigenous to Europe (Juaristi et al. 2008), with some 40 to 50 million EU citizens speaking about 60 of them (European Commission 2012, 2; European Commission/EACEA/Eurydice 2017, 48). It is also estimated that "at least 175 nationalities are now present within the EU's borders," and certainly a similar number of migrant languages, too (European Union 2018). In 2018, there were 22.3 million non-EU citizens living in the EU – these numbers do not include all those speakers of non-official EU languages who might have acquired EU citizenship (Eurostat 2019, 9).

The pecking order among the languages spoken in the EU begins with the 24 official and working languages – with an abyss between English and the other 23, as addressed in Chapter 3. Increasingly, the other 23 are perceived as minority languages in relation to English (see Nic Craith 2006, 67; Nic Shuibhne 2008,

DOI: 10.4324/9781003342069-4

Table 4.1 The four dimensions of minority languages spoken in EU territory

1 *Official EU languages minus English*
   Bulgarian • Croatian • Czech • Danish • Dutch • Estonian • Finnish • French • German • Greek • Hungarian • Irish • Italian • Latvian • Lithuanian • Maltese • Polish • Portuguese • Romanian • Slovak • Slovenian • Spanish • Swedish
2 *European territorial languages*
   Albanian • Arabic, Cypriot Maronite • Aragonese • Aranese • Armenian • Aromanian (Vlach) • Asturian • Basque • Belarusian • Bosnian • Breton • Catalan • Corsican • Faroese • Frisian • Frisian, North • Frisian, Sater • Frisian, West • Friulian • Galician • German, Low • Greenlandic • Hebrew • Istro-Romanian • Karaim • Kashubian • Ladin • Latgalian • Lemko • Leonese • Limburgish • Livonian[1] • Macedonian • Meänkieli • Mirandés • Montenegrin • Occitan • Russian • Ruthenian • Sardinian • Saxon, Lower • Scanian • Serbian • Sorbian, Lower • Sorbian, Upper • Tamazight (Berber)[2] • Tatar • Tatar, Crimean • Turkish • Ukrainian • Valencian
3 *European non-territorial languages*
   Beás • Karelian • Romani (Romany, Romanes, Romani Chib) • Sámi, Eastern/Skolt • Sámi, Inari • Sámi, Lule • Sámi, North • Sámi, South • Yiddish
4 *Migrant languages*
   Arabic, Algerian • Berber, Kabyle • Chinese • Gujarati • Hindi / Urdu • Punjabi • Russian • Tunisian

Sign languages – most national and regional languages depicted here, plus additional varieties (e.g., French from France, Belgium and Switzerland).

Sources: For rows two and three: the list of languages included in the European Charter for Regional or Minority Languages (ECRML) (of January 2018 – see www.coe.int/en/web/european-charter-regional-or-minority-languages) and the European Commission's interactive map of regional and minority languages (of December 2019 – see www.map.language-diversity.eu/). Rows two and three feature a comprehensive, though not exhaustive, list of languages. Row four includes a small sample of languages.

[1] The last native speaker of Livonian is reported to have died in 2013 in Canada (Charter 2013). However, the European Commission's interactive map of regional and minority languages lists 135 speakers in Western Latvia. The language does not feature in the ECRML because Latvia is not among the signatories (more below).
[2] Tamazight, a variety of Berber, is only listed in the European Commission's interactive map of regional and minority languages because of Melilla, the Spanish autonomous city in the Northwest coast of Africa. Berber varieties are spoken by millions of people with Moroccan and Algerian background in Belgium, France, Germany, Italy, the Netherlands and Spain, but are not included in either map as they are not considered indigenous to Europe.

124). The second "level" is that of the EU's 60-something allochthonous languages, such as Catalan and Frisian, which may or may not be protected by the ECRML, and whose speakers may or may not enjoy special rights in the regions where they live.

Non-territorial European languages, such as the Sámi and Romani languages, comprise "level" three. As noted in Chapter 1, some of these languages enjoy some *de jure* protections in a number of member states, thanks mainly to the ECRML. Recent estimates set the number of Romani speakers alone living in Europe at 10–12 million (European Commission 2020, 1).

Finally, the fourth "level" encompasses allochthonous languages, i.e., non-indigenous, migrant languages, such as Arabic. The issue of the distinction between autochthonous and allochthonous languages, addressed in Chapter 1 in the context of the ECRML, is crucial to the present chapter. This terminology hallowed by custom was borrowed from biology and is unfortunate because it suggests an original, primeval link between these languages and the territories in which they are spoken. The next link, namely with ethnicities, is only a short step away. We must also ask ourselves how long a language must have been present in how large a portion of a territory for it to be considered indigenous or autochthonous (see, e.g., Edwards 2013, 9; Leal 2021, 80).

Sign languages constitute a separate category here – both indigenous to Europe and territorial, their status and that of their speakers vary greatly from member state to member state. As is the case with policy pertaining to spoken languages, sign language policy lies outside the EU's jurisdiction, so the EU may neither enforce new, nor harmonise existing, legislation in this area. Having provisions for sign languages to be used as medium of instruction in schools, thus guaranteeing inclusive education, is one of the most pressing issues facing the EU today in the area of education. Yet the lack of EU-wide, overarching policies means that these communities cannot rely on a transnational institutional apparatus to have their claims heard. Table 4.2 illustrates these disparities within the bloc, with some sign languages attaining some kind of legal recognition in their respective states in the 1980s, others in the 2020s, and others not at all. The reader will notice, for example, that France is the only EU member state that does not feature in Table 4.2.[1]

Table 4.2 Sign languages in the EU (January 2022)

Country	Year of Sign Language Recognition
Austria	2005
Belgium	2003, 2006 and 2019
Bulgaria	2021
Croatia	2015
Cyprus	2006
Czech Republic	1998 and 2008
Denmark	2014
Estonia	2007
Finland	1995
Germany	2002
Greece	2017
Hungary	2009
Ireland	2017
Italy	2021
Latvia	1999
Lithuania	1995
Luxembourg	2018
Malta	2016
Netherlands	2020
Poland	2011
Portugal	1997
Romania	2002
Slovakia	1995
Slovenia	2002
Spain	2007 and 2010
Sweden	1981, 2006 and 2009

Source: https://wfdeaf.org/news/the-legal-recognition-of-national-sign-languages/ (last accessed in December 2022).

There is surprisingly little information on migrant languages in the EU – though perhaps this is not so surprising in view of the fact that there is little information on the language practices and ideologies of EU citizens as a whole, whether their languages are official, autochthonous or allochthonous, signed or spoken. In fact, there also seems to be relatively little research on migrant languages and their speakers (Pérez-Izaguirre et al. 2022). EU-wide data is hard to come by, but regions and especially cities do often collect statistics on language use. This highlights the need, voiced by Ó Riain in this chapter's interview, to address language matters at the level of the Commission. Within the framework of the threefold turn for the EU detailed in Chapter 3, the creation of a pluricentric agency for language policy and planning, bridging the Directorate-General for Translation (DGT) and the Commission's representations in the member states, constitutes a key step in this direction. The representations could both map existing and collect new data on the language policies, practices and ideologies of their respective member states, feeding this data into a transnational database managed by DGT, thus generating EU-wide statistics.

The question of migrant and non-territorial languages dovetails with the issue of EU citizenship; both are hugely symbolic as they highlight that this community – this union – has an inside and an outside. Jacques Derrida, perhaps one of the most insightful philosophers of the notion of "community" in Western philosophy, cautions against our yearning for forming communities, for they inexorably entail establishing exclusionary mechanisms (Derrida 1998, 355 – translated by Peggy Kamuf):

> I don't much like the word community. (...) If by community one implies, as it is often the case, a harmonious group, consensus and fundamental agreement beneath the phenomena of discord and war, then I don't believe in it very much and I sense in it as much threat as promise. There is doubtless this irrepressible desire for a "community" to form, but also for it to know its limit – and for its limit to be its opening.

Looking at the EU through the lens of Derrida's deconstruction can illuminate the bloc's innermost dilemmas from unexpected angles. One of the many definitions of deconstruction is the very "preparation for the incoming of the other" (Caputo & Derrida 1997, 108 – see Leal 2014, 303). This "other" can be understood in terms of the levels presented in Table 4.1, with that of migrants constituting the "outermost other."

At first glance, what looks like an inclusive community in which state boundaries are lifted and the notion of national, state-bound citizenship is taken to the supranational level, can also be seen as a mechanism of internal exclusion on historical, linguistic and ethnic grounds (Leal 2021, 54). As noted in Chapter 1, Joshua A. Fishman remarks that the EU "has [not] made any effort whatsoever to extend any rights or courtesies to [its] manifold immigrant languages" (2006, 314). For Étienne Balibar, this is first and foremost a question of citizenship. In fact, he speaks of a "virtual European apartheid" in this respect, as "the other face of the development of the European Union and its quest for identity" (2004, x, 65). In his view, the EU's democratic deficit is a consequence of its treatment of citizenship. To overcome or reverse this deficit, he argues that the EU must become *more* democratic than the member states, and that this democratic surplus must be accessible to all who "'happen' to live and therefore work, bear children, support relatives, find partners for every sort of 'intercourse'" in the member states (Balibar 2004, 132). In his view, the EU's problematic and conflicted stance on citizenship will block "European unification as a democratic construction" (Balibar 2004, 170).

As we will see in this chapter's interview, Ó Riain believes that the notion of "parity of esteem" can help placate these issues of citizenship and language in the EU. Whichever form parity of esteem may take – whether symbolic or concrete – it represents a key step towards a workable kind of equality. When it comes to languages, we must distinguish between at least two types of equality, namely equality of *status* and equality in *use*. Twenty-four languages enjoy equality of status in the EU as official *and* working languages. This begs the question whether languages beyond these autochthonous, national languages should be granted EU official status – a question to which we will return in the commentary below and in Chapter 5.

Equality in *use*, in turn, is about *de facto* multilingualism in EU institutions, bodies and agencies. It would be unrealistic to expect, say, Italian to be used as often as, say, Maltese in both written and oral communication in the EU. Perhaps we ought to replace the notion of equality in use by the concept of *aimed equity* – because *total* equity would be impossible. Ideological and physical space must be carved out in the EU so that aimed equity can be striven for. Status equality should not prevent the EU from acknowledging the differences (in meaning and in use) among these languages (Leal 2021, 115).

Equality of status and use dovetails with the question of "parity of esteem" raised in the interview below. Parity of esteem played a pivotal part in the Good Friday Agreement (1998), as noted by Ó Riain. Article 1, paragraph v, stipulates that "the power of the sovereign government (...) shall be founded on the principles of parity of esteem and of just and equal treatment for the identity, ethos and aspirations of both communities." When it comes to languages, in Ireland as in the EU, it is impossible to look at parity of esteem as a question of symbolic status devoid of the practical dimension of equality in use, or aimed equity, as suggested above. Let us turn to the interview now – we will come back to the issue of the Irish language in Chapter 6.

Interview

9 *An urgent and controversial issue addressed in previous chapters pertains to migrant languages in Europe. There are dozens of migrant languages here, whose communities are often larger than those of some of the official EU languages. Linguistic segregation is widespread, for example, in EU schools, and since language policy is not an EU area of competence, no overarching framework can be designed, nor can local legislation be harmonised. Should these language communities be granted specific rights?*
A. Yes, this question addresses a major weakness in European integration – the fact that language policy, culture and education is an exclusively national competence. Many would not agree that this important area should be Europeanised, but surely there is an argument for at least mixed competence, as a common European element in education should reflect our common history and culture. The fact that we in Europe have so much in common, we have evolved over centuries, it should be possible to teach a common element of European history, to help children see their national histories in a European context.

One of the main functions of the European Commission is to represent the general European interest. The Commissioners swear an oath that they will not take instructions from any national government. Is there not a general European interest in the linguistic and cultural area? In areas like competition and trade, where a European competence has been recognised, there is huge progress. On the other hand, areas such as language, culture and education remain at point zero – there are some recommendations occasionally, but these are easily ignored.

At present the Conference on the future of Europe is seeking the views of citizens. Some countries are open to treaty change, if needed, whereas others are not, as they see it as time-consuming,

Migrant and non-territorial languages in the EU 99

and that it would be difficult to get agreement among 27 countries. I think that we do need to be open to treaty change, particularly in adding a European competence to the linguistic, cultural and educational area, moving away from exclusively member state competence. Turning to migrant languages, and the cultural area in general, overall EU policies could then be framed in a mixed committee by representatives of all the national ministries of education, with a Commission representative, so that the general European context could also be taken into account in all decisions. I think this is extremely important.

10 *European non-territorial languages also have sizeable communities of speakers who are often vulnerable – a recent EU report on the Roma population reveals that discrimination is rampant across the bloc. Yet the report does not mention language at all. The ECRML excludes non-territorial languages because a territorial base is a prerequisite for the Charter to work. However, it does encourage that all autochthonous languages spoken in a given state – whether territorial or not – be granted specific rights. How can these communities be protected, and these languages fostered?*
A. Migrant languages and Roma languages and other non-territorial languages are also languages with their own tradition and need to be valued. There is a question, of course, as to how far a state can go. For instance, we did discuss this in the Council of Europe ECRML committee, and a colleague pointed out that there were over 350 languages spoken as native languages in London alone. There would be clear practical difficulties in offering services in so many languages. It should be possible, however, to encourage the study of all languages and to maintain and strengthen immigrants' links with their home countries. This is becoming easier in a more digitalised world.

Regarding both migrant and non-territorial languages, however, I see a possible role for a neutral language like Esperanto, which would prevent the strong imposing their language on the weak. The Roma are usually a small minority; frequently they are not the most respected community in an area, and you often get the local community imposing their language on them. A role for a neutral language like Esperanto would show that those who speak Roma, or other non-territorial languages or migrant languages, are of equal value with members of the majority community.

That would be clear if representatives of the majority community dealing with migrants were to make the effort to study a neutral language, designed to be easy, to communicate with them. That would be meeting them halfway. It would, of course, be important to show that short Esperanto courses can speed up subsequent language learning, and thus can actually save time. As this is counter-intuitive, but true, it is difficult to get across.

I see an analogy with industrial relations, where both employers and trade unions agree to meet in arbitration – a halfway house. Why not apply this concept to the linguistic area, instead of allowing the strong to impose their language on the weak? I say that as an Irish speaker. We had over seven centuries of a very strong neighbour imposing its language on us and telling us that our language was worthless and should be forgotten. When people shake hands, each person extends their hand, and they meet halfway. Esperanto is essentially a linguistic handshake, where mutual respect is fundamental.

Such mutual respect led to real progress in Northern Ireland, through the new phrase "parity of esteem." Traditionally you had a Protestant British community, which was dominant for 50 years or more, and a minority Catholic, Irish nationalist community, which met with discrimination in areas such as housing and jobs. The Irish element was seen as undesirable in a Northern Ireland which aimed to be exclusively British and Protestant. This never worked, as the Catholic minority was too large, and tended to have more children. Far from disappearing, it is now close to making up the majority of the community in Northern Ireland.

The key to a solution was this ingenious phrase "parity of esteem." It was invented by a colleague of mine, former ambassador Seán Ó Huiginn, with whom I worked in Berlin. The two communities are not equally wealthy, they are not equal in numbers, but they are entitled to parity of esteem, the same amount of respect as the other. The flag, anthem and traditions of one community are to be seen as of equal value as the flag, anthem and traditions of the other community. This entailed an international treaty between the UK and Ireland, and new constitutional arrangements in Ireland. Everybody born in Northern Ireland is entitled to Irish or British nationality, or both. They can legally have two nationalities, two passports, one Irish and one British. There was no longer an imposition on either community

Migrant and non-territorial languages in the EU 101

of the identities or the symbols of the other community. "Parity of esteem" has produced the relative peace of the last 20 years, following the Good Friday Agreement, which was accepted by referendum in May 1998 by huge majorities in both parts of Ireland. It was the first time since 1918 that all of Ireland voted on the same issue on the same day.

In the language area in Europe, you have a real need for parity of esteem. As a native English speaker, I fail to see why I should have an automatic, lifelong, unfair advantage over the 99 per cent of EU citizens who do not have English as their native language. It appears unfair and unjust – not the best basis on which to build European integration.

Commentary

One of the key issues that emerged in the interview is that of linguistic justice. As addressed in the previous chapters, there are numerous linguistic injustices at the level of the EU official languages (see Table 4.1 above), particularly as regards the chasm between English and the other 23. This issue is exacerbated as we move down Table 4.1, from the official languages to the indigenous European languages, the non-territorial languages and the migrant languages (with sign languages featuring somewhere between these levels).

There are different models of linguistic justice that can be applied to the EU. Let us focus on two opposing models here, which may help to predict in which direction the EU's language hierarchy is going to develop in the medium and long terms. François Grin's model is grounded in five key clusters of injustices in the EU in relation to English, as displayed in Table 4.3. As mentioned in Chapter 2, he estimates that these injustices amounted to profits worth €17 billion flowing from the EU into the UK in 2005 alone – a "conservative estimate," he adds (Grin 2008, 80).

Due to space constraints, let us unpack two of these five injustices, namely "knock-on effects" and "legitimisation effects." If we take school curricula, Grin explains that continental European countries (2015, 133–134)

> typically teach two foreign languages to 95% of their schoolgoing population. The corresponding expenditure averages 10%

of total educational spending (…) By having largely abandoned the requirement for schools to teach foreign languages at all, the English education system (…) saves roughly 6% of total spending. This, of course, is at the expense of learners of English, in Europe and beyond, who learn it as a foreign or second language, at significant public, and often private, expense.

Schools in England can hence allocate these resources – financial, intellectual, logistical, etc. – elsewhere, while being assured that continental Europe will invest in English teaching, translation, interpreting, etc.

As for "legitimisation effects," Grin posits that quantification is impossible, but these constitute the most significant injustice – and others confirm this (see, e.g., Ostler 2010, 25). Native-born Anglophones are often overrepresented in key positions across large enterprises and international organisations. As noted in Chapter 2, in 2010, 42 per cent of the EU commissioners' spokespersons were

Table 4.3 Transfers enjoyed by native speakers of English

1	Privileged markets	Quasi monopoly over translation/interpreting and English teaching branches, including exchange programmes, materials, etc.
2	Communication savings effort	No translation/interpreting expenditure for native speakers as non-natives make the effort and financial investment to learn English
3	Language learning savings effort	Because English is so widely spoken, native speakers do not need to invest the time and money into learning additional languages
4	Knock-on effects	Time and resources allocated to translation/interpreting services, language learning and foreign language teaching (e.g., in school curricula) can be devoted to something else
5	Legitimisation effects	Native speakers are almost always in a better position to control the agenda, negotiate, influence others etc. as their language "carries intrinsic legitimization"

Source: Based on Grin (2015, 132–134). Taken from Leal (2021, 148).

Migrant and non-territorial languages in the EU 103

native speakers of English (Grin 2015, 134–135). The distributive effects of the dominant position of English are the crux of the matter: the benefits enjoyed by inner-circle nations exceed the weight of its population and generate linguistic injustices, which, in turn, translate into financial, social and political injustices (Leal 2021, 149).

As a steadfast defender of multilingualism, Grin proposes different strategies to counteract the hegemony of English and promote linguistic justice in the EU, namely maintaining equality of status among EU languages and the concomitant translation/interpreting services; adopting Esperanto (e.g., Grin 2008, 2011); and fostering receptive competences and intercomprehension skills within the bloc (e.g., Grin 2011). Above all, he highlights the need for a complex set of well-coordinated measures in which English also plays a part (see Leal 2021, 149). However, Grin takes the inequalities entailed in the EU's translation and interpreting regimes for granted (see Chapter 3 and Leal 2021, 149); nor does he approach the more unrealistic aspects of the introduction of Esperanto into the EU's linguistic *modus operandi*, listed in the previous chapters.

An opposing model here is the one by Philippe Van Parijs which, in fact, departs from a similar notion of linguistic justice, yet arrives at radically different solutions – as noted in Chapter 2. Van Parijs wrote what seems to be the first-ever monograph on linguistic justice in 2011 (De Schutter 2018, 168), in which he identifies three types of linguistic injustice, as displayed in Table 4.4. He concedes that all three clusters of injustices afflict speakers of all languages other than English in the EU, and perhaps for this reason he arrives at the conclusion that the solution lies in democratising and universalising access to high quality English teaching across the globe – as his model is not restricted to the EU. A strong motivating factor for Van Parijs's campaign to promote English is his claim that a significant portion of the world's population *already speaks it* – to an extent that is not comparable to any other language today or in the past.

Grim forecasts of the fate of English in the short and medium terms notwithstanding (Graddol 2006; Ostler 2010), Van Parijs contends that whichever measures would be needed now to compensate for the dominance of English would become obsolete once every person on the planet is fluent in it. Unlike Grin, Van Parijs

Table 4.4 Linguistic injustice

1	Cooperative injustice	The effortless, costless benefits enjoyed by native speakers thanks to the learning efforts of non-natives
2	Distributive injustice	Increased opportunities and financial gains to native speakers given the increased value of their mother tongue
3	Disparity of esteem	The more privileged position of native speakers to the detriment of non-natives and the concomitant effect on one's self-esteem and dignity

Source: Based on Van Parijs (2011). Taken from Leal (2021, 145).

is not a defender of multilingualism for the intrinsic or expressive value of languages, nor does he take into account the factors that persuade, compel and at times coerce communities to stop speaking a given language in favour of another.

This is not the place to recount the acrimonious debate that followed the publication of Van Parijs's model of linguistic justice and which still reverberates through multiple disciplines. For our purposes here, the focal point is the value of linguistic diversity – or lack thereof. In places such as the EU, in which an ever-growing portion of the population share a second language, and the "national language plus English" model dominates, the territoriality principle becomes tricky (Van Parijs 2008, 37). As "local linguistic diversity" increases with the addition of English to a people's repertoire, "inter-local diversity" decreases as various peoples speak the same lingua franca and this gradually brings people's languages closer through language contact (Van Parijs 2011, 185–188). In this scenario, all languages other than the lingua franca become minority languages which, in turn, pushes today's minority languages (i.e., regional, non-territorial, migrant and sign languages, or any languages that do not enjoy territorial majority) over the edge of the cliff as collateral damage. Van Parijs's model admittedly damages local diversity in the long run as well, as implementing the territoriality principle may secure some inter-local diversity at the expense of local diversity (see, e.g., De Schutter & Robichaud 2015, 103–104 – see Leal 2021, 146–147).

Van Parijs hypothesises that, were the EU to lift the territoriality principle, this would "amount to nothing more terrible than turning the whole planet into a large number of Republics of Ireland, with only vestiges of the local languages (...) and with a somewhat idiosyncratic way of pronouncing the lingua franca, now promoted to mother tongue status," as quoted in Chapter 2 (2015, 242). This would, however, be at odds with the current language policies, discourse and ideologies in the EU (see Leal 2023). Different Eurobarometer surveys reveal that EU citizens value linguistic diversity and the equal treatment among EU languages (see, e.g., European Commission 2012). EU language policy (see Chapter 2) goes hand in glove with its discourse on language in non-legally binding documents; in other words, both celebrate multilingualism clearly and univocally. This suggests a conflicted scenario as regards language ideologies, as both EU institutions, bodies and agencies *and* EU citizens seem torn between a deep appreciation of their languages, on the one hand, and the desire for a common language for pragmatic reasons, on the other. To complicate matters further, citizenship criteria across the EU require language proficiency, suggesting that this appreciation of language is rather limited – it applies to the national language in its territory.

This leaves all languages beyond the national languages in a precarious situation – particularly sign, migrant and non-territorial languages. Could Esperanto act as a bridge, as suggested by Ó Riain – a token of parity of esteem, a gesture of goodwill or halfway meeting point? In previous chapters, we addressed the question of a need for a shift in mentality, particularly in terms of our expectations of a certain geographical, cultural and sociopolitical boundedness of language which simply does not apply to Esperanto in the same way that it does to the languages of Europe. Another shift would be necessary in this context, too, namely regarding myths surrounding language acquisition. I do not have any thorough statistics at hand, but bringing up my children in three languages has meant that I am often confronted with the view that individual multilingualism confuses children, reduces their skills in and knowledge of their languages and makes learning additional languages more difficult. In fact, we know today that the opposite applies in all three instances (see, e.g., Edwards 2013; Fürst & Grin 2018), but it may be some time before this awareness comes to shape mainstream views on language.

Persuading Europeans that learning an additional language – which by the way is not the official language of any state – is necessary to better welcome immigrants, and persuading immigrants that they should invest in learning an additional language before devoting themselves to the national language plus English, is a tall order. Both sides would likely opine that introducing a third language – beyond the national language and English – complicates and retards the truly necessary step of learning the national language plus English. This is, of course, an unfounded opinion, but language practices do not lend themselves to top-down measures which do not reflect existing language practices and ideologies – at least to a certain extent.

This leaves us with the question of whether migrant and non-territorial languages should enjoy some kind of differentiated EU status and protections. Perhaps Balibar is right and therein lies the new model of citizenship to reinvent the EU and placate the democratic deficit. Or perhaps official EU status, a topic to which we will return in Chapter 5, would not be needed if these languages, their communities and interests were protected through, for example, an EU agency for language policy and planning.

Note

1 I would like to thank Natasha Parkins-Maliko for recommending sources in the area of sign languages.

References

Balibar, Étienne. 2004. *We, the people of Europe: Reflections on transnational citizenship*. Princeton & Oxford: Princeton University Press.

Caputo, John, and Jacques Derrida. 1997. *Deconstruction in a nutshell: A conversation with Jacques Derrida*. New York: Fordham University Press.

De Schutter, Helder. 2018. "Linguistic justice and English as a Lingua Franca." In *The politics of multilingualism: Europeanisation, globalisation and linguistic governance*, 167–199. Amsterdam & Philadelphia: John Benjamins.

De Schutter, Helder, and David Robichaud. 2015. "Van Parijsian linguistic justice – context, analysis and critiques." *Critical Review of International Social and Political Philosophy* 18 (2): 87–112.

Derrida, Jacques. 1998. *Points ... Interviews, 1974–1994*. Edited by Elizabeth Weber. Translated by Peggy Kamuf. Stanford: Stanford University Press.

Edwards, John. 2013. "Bilingualism and multilingualism: Some central concepts." In *The handbook of bilingualism and multilingualism*, edited by Tej K. Bhatia and William C. Ritchie, 6–25. Malden: Blackwell Publishing.
European Commission. 2012. "Special Eurobarometer 386: Europeans and their languages." https://ec.europa.eu/commfrontoffice/publicopinion/archives/ebs/ebs_386_en.pdf.
European Commission. 2020. "EU Roma strategic framework for equality, inclusion and participation for 2020 – 2030." https://ec.europa.eu/info/sites/info/files/union_of_equality_eu_roma_strategic_framework_for_equality_inclusion_and_participation_en.pdf.
European Commission/EACEA/Eurydice. 2017. *Key data on teaching languages at school in Europe: Eurydice report.* Luxembourg: Publications Office of the European Union.
European Union. 2018. *European days of languages 2018.* https://europa.eu/cultural-heritage/node/699_en.html.
Eurostat. 2019. *Migration and migrant population statistics.* European Union. https://ec.europa.eu/eurostat/statistics-explained/pdfscache/1275.pdf.
Fishman, Joshua A. 2006. "Language policy and language shift." In *An introduction to language policy: Theory and method*, edited by Thomas Ricento, 311–328. Malden: Blackwell Publishing.
Fürst, Guillaume, and François Grin. 2018. "Are multilingual individuals more creative?" In *Mobility and inclusion in multilingual Europe: The MIME Vademecum*, edited by François Grin, 170–171.
Graddol, David. 2006. *English next: Why global English may mean the end of 'English as a Foreign Language'.* London: British Council.
Grin, François. 2008. "Principles of policy evaluation and their application to multilingualism in the European Union." In *Respecting linguistic diversity in the European Union*, edited by Xabier Arzoz, 73–83. Amsterdam & Philadelphia: John Benjamins.
Grin, François, interview by European Commission. 2011. *Lingua franca: Chimera or reality?* 59–70.
Grin, François. 2015. "The economics of English in Europe." In *Language policy and political economy: English in a global context*, edited by Thomas Ricento, 119–144. Oxford: Oxford University Press.
Juaristi, Patxi, Timothy Reagan, and Humphrey Tonkin. 2008. "Linguistic diversity in the European Union: An overview." In *Respecting linguistic diversity in the European Union*, edited by Xabier Arzoz, 47–72. Amsterdam & Philadelphia: John Benjamins.
Leal, Alice. 2014. *Is the glass half empty or half full? Reflections on translation theory and practice in Brazil.* Berlin: Frank & Timme.

Leal, Alice. 2021. *English and translation in the European Union: Unity and multiplicity in the wake of Brexit.* Abingdon & New York: Routledge.
Leal, Alice. 2023. "Meaningful diversity in the European Union: Multilingualism and the pull of English as a 'lingua franca'." In *Diversity & inclusion across languages: Insights into communicative challenges from theory and practice,* edited by Bernadette Hofer-Bonfim, Elisabeth Peters, Johannes Schnitzer and Magdalena Zehetgruber, 31–46. Berlin: Frank & Timme.
Nic Craith, Máiréad. 2006. *Europe and the politics of language: Citizens, migrants and outsiders.* New York: Palgrave Macmillan.
Nic Shuibhne, Niamh. 2008. "EC law and minority language policy: Some recent developments." In *Respecting linguistic diversity in the European Union,* edited by Xabier Arzoz, 123–143. Amsterdam & Philadelphia: John Benjamins.
Ostler, Nicholas. 2010. *The last lingua franca: The rise and fall of world languages.* London: Penquin Books.
Pérez-Izaguirre, Elizabeth, Gorka Roman, and María Orcasitas-Vicandi. 2022. "Immigrant minority languages and multilingual education in Europe: A literature review." *International Journal of Multilingualism.* doi:10.1080/14790718.2022.2121401.
Van Parijs, Philippe. 2008. "Linguistic diversity as curse and as by-product." In *Respecting linguistic diversity in the European Union,* edited by Xabier Arzoz, 17–46. Amsterdam & Philadelphia: John Benjamins.
Van Parijs, Philippe. 2011. *Linguistic justice for Europe and for the world.* Oxford: Oxford University Press.
Van Parijs, Philippe. 2015. "The ground floor of the world: On the socio-economic consequences of linguistic globalization." In *Language policy and political economy: English in a global context,* edited by Thomas Ricento, 231–251. Oxford: Oxford University Press.

5 Language policy and official EU status

Introductory remarks

Many of the issues discussed in the previous chapters revolve around the notion of official EU status, itself a reflection of the EU's legal and institutional framework in terms of the division of competences between the transnational and the national level. This chapter presents a discussion about whether language policy should remain a prerogative of the member states or whether it should not rather become a shared competence; a reflection on the formation of the EU and its changing priorities over the years; a suggestion of the possible need for a treaty change in this area; a critical appraisal of the impact of EU status for languages such as Irish vis-à-vis others (e.g. Catalan); a discussion of the importance of top-down language policy to protect multilingualism; an analysis of the role of English in the EU, both official and unofficial, in the wake of Brexit; and a critical appraisal of the differences among EU regional and minority languages.

In this chapter's interview, Ó Riain comments on the formation of the EU as the merging of France's and Germany's coal and steel industries to prevent war – an economic union, as it were, as a peacekeeping endeavour. Indeed, as argued elsewhere (Leal 2021, 128–133) and noted in Chapter 2, the Treaty establishing the European Coal and Steel Community (1951) showcases these two dimensions prominently (i.e., peace and economic development) but also includes a third dimension, namely that of a shared destiny. It is beyond doubt that the EU has succeeded as regards peace and economic development, two colossal achievements often taken for granted in contemporary appraisals of the EU. But has it engendered a sense of shared destiny among its citizens?

The question of a European identity, addressed several times in the previous chapters, encapsulates this conundrum of a shared destiny. Perhaps we ought to replace the notion of European identity – fraught as it is with controversy from the outset – by the concept of shared fate or destiny. This shared destiny should not be understood in the Heideggerian sense of a community of destiny (see Balibar 2014, 144), but rather along the lines of what Herman van Gunsteren calls "communities of fate," and Melissa Williams calls "communities of shared fate." In other words, the point is *not* to have some kind of common national, ethnical, cultural or linguistic identity in some ideal future; the point is rather that there *already exist* "relations of interdependence that may or may not be positively valued" (Williams 2004, 104), and which, in practical terms, mean that the members of these communities "cannot avoid each other without depriving themselves of what is essential for their way of life (for instance, water supply, a viable economy, institutions of learning, military protection, a judicial system, and territory)" (van Gunsteren 2018, 61). We will come back to this question in the commentary below.

Language policy remains a prerogative of the member states as the predominant view is that language is too entangled with issues of national identity, nationhood and sovereignty for Brussels to have any influence over it. Ó Riain stresses that changes can be engendered in the cultural and linguistic realms without the need for treaty change – though he does leave a door open for treaty change. While it is clear that more substantial changes, such as adding or removing a language, should be predicated on consensus decisions, less drastic measures can be taken within the existing legislative framework – such as the creation of a pluricentric agency for language policy and planning.

The EU has been gradually moving away from the unanimity model anyway – a shift that has been intensified by the pandemic and the invasion of Ukraine. The Treaty of Lisbon (2009) already increased the number of policy areas requiring qualified majority rather than consensus. It also introduced the so-called "passarelle clauses," which allow certain legislative procedures that require unanimity to be settled on qualified majority voting. Passarelle clauses make decision-making swifter and more flexible, particularly with a view to an ever-expanding EU, which could reach 30 members in the foreseeable future (Moldova, Ukraine and Bosnia and Herzegovina were granted the status of candidate states in 2022, following Turkey (1999), North Macedonia (2005), Montenegro (2010), Serbia (2012) and Albania (2014)).

The caveat is that unanimity is required to allow for passarelle clauses to be implemented in the first place, and consensus is not in sight. The current rift between the EU and Hungary regarding, among other issues, sanctions against Russia in the aftermath of the invasion of Ukraine epitomises this quandary. This notwithstanding, one of the main outcomes of the Conference on the future of Europe has been the call for a far-reaching transition to qualified majority voting, so it may be realistic to expect significant changes to be introduced soon (see, e.g., Mintel & von Ondarza 2022).

A shift from a consensus mentality, coupled with a heightened awareness of the need for the cultural and linguistic realm to be fostered in the EU, may provide more fertile ground for the threefold turn mentioned in the previous chapters to flourish – without requiring treaty change. Here, a key question in the context of the number of official EU languages – raised by Ó Riain in this chapter's interview – is that of the concomitant costs of language services. Hasty journalistic and academic appraisals thereof notwithstanding, the EU's language services, comprising translation and interpreting in *24 languages*, do not cost much – about 1 per cent of the EU's total budget, or €2.20 per citizen annually. In contrast, Canadian citizens contribute around €36 a year to keep their federal services *bilingual* (Gazzola 2014, 232 – based on Vaillancourt & Coche). It must also be noted that scrapping or reducing the EU's language services would not entail a cut, but rather a *transfer* of the costs to the national level (Gazzola & Grin 2013, 103–104 – see Leal 2022).

Ó Riain raises this point in relation to the recent end of the derogation period in which the Irish language had been placed in 2007, and the subsequent increase in the demand for language services involving Irish in the EU (see Chapter 2) – which on his account some see as wasteful. Ireland's linguistic landscape remains unparalleled in Europe and perhaps beyond the continent as well. Its national and first official language, Irish, is spoken at home by a minority – the 2016 census lists 73,803 daily Irish speakers outside school, down from 77,185 in 2011.[1] Its second official language, English – introduced in the country as a colonial language in an ostensive campaign against Irish – is spoken pretty much by all. Much like the question of *whether* a shift from English to Irish can be brought about today, the question of *how* the shift from Irish to English took place is complex. It can be understood as

> ... the cumulative effect of colonisation, plantation and suppression, particularly from the 16th century onwards, [leading] to the elimination of the Irish-speaking aristocracy and their institutions. Additionally, catastrophic famine, emigration and epidemics decimated the Irish-speaking rural indigenous population during the 19th century, all factors which led to a language shift to English.
> (Mercator European Research Centre on Multilingualism and Language Learning 2016, 5)

The report additionally states, on the same page, that "[l]anguage restoration efforts by voluntary organisations began in the early 20th century," and these efforts "developed into an official policy by the native government after political settlements."[2] The role that official EU status has played in the path towards "restoration" is addressed in this chapter's interview. We cannot overestimate the value of official status, which, alone, just like top-down language policy alone, does not automatically lead to increased incentives and opportunities to use languages, thus translating into renewed language practices.

The world is not short of examples of languages which, despite enjoying official status, are in a position of severe subjugation in the country in question. Witness, for example, the low societal status of – albeit official – Arabic in Israel in relation to the prestige of – albeit non-official – English in the same country (Shohamy 2006, 72).[3] Official status does, however, frequently entail the allocation of resources to these languages which, in turn, has the potential to raise their status and prestige in their respective communities – a factor confirmed by Ó Riain in relation to Irish. In the EU, official status also presents an opportunity for less used languages to be further developed, as their corpora are expanded in a range of written instruments whose production is subsidised by the EU (Arzoz 2008, 6 – see Leal 2021, 80). Official status also entails an increase and improvement in translator and interpreter training, thereby raising the profile of the language in tertiary education. Ireland's diglossia illustrates the difficulties that arise when two languages play a higher and a lower role within the same community. Though already widely used in French Hellenistic studies (see Phillipson 2003, 83), the concept of diglossia became well known in English in the mid-twentieth century, in the writings of Charles A. Ferguson. On Ferguson's terms, "diglossia" referred to two varieties of the same language spoken in a given territory, such as Modern Standard Arabic and local varieties of Arabic. Joshua A. Fishman then proposed the notion of "extended diglossia," i.e., when two genetically unrelated languages play a "higher" and a "lower" role within the same community, such as French and Basque, respectively, in France (see Fishman 1967; Spolsky 2004, 134; Kraus 2008, 101; Leal 2021, 170).

Some of the views reported by Ó Riain in what follows confirm that, for some Irish people, the Irish language has no practical value – it is on the "lower" ground in relation to English as regards language use and number of speakers.[4] As we read about these views, I ask the reader to keep the theory of options and ligatures in mind, mentioned in Chapter 1. Developed by Ralf Dahrendorf in 1979, the theory is based on the fact that our life chances – in the Weberian sense of opportunities to improve our lives – are contingent on a certain balance between our emotional ties or bonds ("ligatures") and the real choices available to us ("options"). Ligatures provide meaning to our actions and positions in society, whereas options determine the framework of possible actions. Dahrendorf warns that "ligatures without options are oppressive, whereas options without bonds are meaningless" (1979, 31 – see Leal 2021, 141–142).

Peter A. Kraus takes this theory and applies it to language. He argues that languages matter to us inasmuch as they establish or they themselves constitute ties, emotional and intellectual bonds to our life-worlds – i.e., ligatures. On the other hand, languages matter to us because of the gates that they open to communities of speakers, goods, privileges, etc. – i.e., options. There can be no zero-sum relationship between the two, but we do strive for a certain balance between our emotional ties to something and what this something actually brings us as regards options to improve our lives (Kraus 2018 – see Leal 2023).

I suggest that there are options that *precede* ligatures and options that *succeed* ligatures. English may well open the most gates today, provide the most options that *succeed* ligatures; yet it also entails the fewest options that *precede* ligatures, because whether or not to adopt is often a non-choice as there is no viable alternative. Through the question of diglossia, the dynamic between options and ligatures becomes evident.

A "higher" language usually entails more options than a "lower" language, in relation to which there are probably more ligatures to begin with. The more options are associated with the "higher" language, the more the allegiances to the "lower" language shift towards the "higher" language. Real, viable opportunities and incentives to use the "lower" language are needed to tip the scales in its favour – even though we know that a zero-sum relationship between "higher" and "lower" languages is impossible (Leal 2021, 142).

The theory of options and ligatures also poses some uncomfortable questions about Irish bilingualism and EU multilingualism: what of this bilingualism / multilingualism (ligatures) without real, legitimate, equally valid and beneficial opportunities to use these languages (options)? When the only viable options remain the member states' official language(s) and, in many realms, only English, then the EU's approach to multilingualism is oppressive, to come back to Dahrendorf (Leal 2021, 142). Let us keep this in mind as we move on to the interview.

Interview

11 *Beneath the surface of the two previous questions about migrant and non-territorial languages lies the EU's disunity and impotence regarding language policy, since it is neither an area of exclusive, shared or supporting competence. From the very outset, the EU was an attempt to find a compromise between the member states' sovereignty (and hence the bloc's intrinsic multiplicity) and the unity that such a supranational grouping requires. Language epitomises this tension between unity versus multiplicity. It is beyond doubt that certain areas of competence should remain a prerogative of the member states – even the boldest federalist dream is well aware of the dangers of a homogenising, teleological, top-down force flowing from Brussels "down" to the member states. But should language policy remain an exclusive prerogative of the member states?*

A. European integration has had major success, in ensuring peace in all EU countries, and in promoting economic development. However, development in the non-economic area is lagging behind. There is a real need to look at questions of identity and language and culture, and the whole idea of strengthening a European identity, a European "we-feeling." European integration concerns the totality of human beings, not just consumers, not only in the economic area. The latter is and will remain extremely important, but other areas need to be added, such as an emotional element, which is lacking at present, the whole idea of creating a stronger European identity in harmony with national and regional identities. Many Europeans simply do not have a European identity; they watch the Olympic Games and they see their own country competing, but not Europe. Therefore, an emotional attachment to Europe is lacking. This is needed to connect the citizen to European integration, and language has a vital role to play in this.

I think in the European area, therefore, we may need to consider treaty change but limited to a very specific area. It should not be controversial to give some competence to the European Union in the area of language and culture, while retaining national competence too. When I worked in the Irish Embassy in Australia, I had the feeling that we were not only representing Ireland, but also the European Union. We have had a number of European treaties, so we should not exclude the idea of treaty change. Such change should be minimised, both in time and in scope.

12 *How important do you think EU official status is for language communities – thinking here for example of Irish, whose community of native speakers is by far the smallest in the EU? And should this numeric criterion play a part at all in the appointment of official languages? Let us think of Catalan here for example, with its over five million speakers.*
A. I agree that EU status has brought huge benefit to Irish. It has been difficult to find the necessary number of interpreters and translators, which is why we needed a temporary derogation. Irish achieved EU status on 1 January 2007 – the decision was taken on 13 June 2005. We needed a unanimous decision by all EU governments, and we achieved this, and are very thankful to the European governments, which all agreed.[5] However, EU status for Irish was controversial in Ireland itself – and it still is to an extent. There are people in Ireland who say that producing all this

material in Irish, which will be little read, is wasteful. They forget that EU regulations and directives in the other languages are normally read only by those directly concerned. We have now about 200 translators and interpreters in Brussels, Luxembourg and Strasbourg, and this will be going up to about 250 because the derogation ends at the end of this year.

There are those who say that this wastes resources, which could be better used. This viewpoint ignores the fact that the EU works as a whole – in the EU institutions the translation services are paid for by the European taxpayer. So, the addition of Irish just adds about €5 cents per citizen per year to the budget. When I worked in DGT, the entire cost of translation into all the languages was about €2 per European per year – the price of a cup of coffee.

The point about the corpus [that official status helps to expand the corpus of minority languages], about helping language to develop precision in vocabulary in new areas, is true and is beneficial to Irish. The problem was never a lack of vocabulary in Irish, but how to reach agreement on one precise term. Professor Tomás de Bhaldraithe once wrote that he had found 18 Irish words for a telescope! But it's the prestige function that counts – the fact that Irish now is one of the official working languages of the EU has given it a prestige at home that it didn't have before. There is now a move to increase its prestige further. The Official Languages Act, passed in 2003, is being strengthened at present – it's before Parliament.[6] The new act should be in force by the end of this year. The Act sets a target that, by 2030, 20 per cent of all public servants would be fluent in the two official languages, English and Irish. This is a huge improvement on the present situation.

The Ministry of Education for many years up to the 1980s actually functioned in Irish. For some reason in the 1980s and 1990s there was a huge decline. About 15 years ago, I remember reading that only 1.5 per cent of those working in the Department of Education were competent to carry out their work in Irish. This led to jokes among the Irish language community that the Irish department of education, *an Roinn Oideachais* should change its name to *an Roinn gan Oideachas*, meaning "the Department without Education!"

There is a real move away from this now. We have had interpretation for many years in the parliament from Irish to English, and not from English to Irish, as it was deemed unnecessary.

I saw statistics on *Dáil Éireann* (the lower house of the Irish parliament) for 2018 – about 20 per cent of politicians have a good knowledge of Irish, about 30 deputies out of 160. However, actual use of Irish in 2018 was 0.5 per cent. In other words, 99.5 per cent of debates in the Irish parliament was conducted in the Queen's English, by Irish nationalists, and 0.5 per cent in the national language.

Last week I read an article that there are now discussions afoot to try to increase the amount of Irish spoken in the parliament tenfold, to bring it from 0.5 per cent up to 5 per cent. There would still be 95 per cent in English, but it would be a huge increase, 10 times as much Irish as at present. This should be possible, as 20 per cent of deputies are able to use Irish. It's an important area because to succeed, you need to set down an actual amount of time per week where using Irish would become the norm, even if only 15 minutes or half an hour per week – e.g., to decide that from 4:30 to 5:00 p.m. every Wednesday afternoon, only Irish will be used. All deputies who do not speak Irish but who wish to contribute at this time, should be provided with an official interpreter. This on its own would increase the practical value of the language. It should not be seen as taking away the rights of English speakers. It is guaranteeing a minimum level of interaction in Irish. The unregulated system for the last century has unduly favoured the stronger language, and it is time to restore some balance.

[To control the agenda a little bit.]

Exactly, to control the agenda. Up to now, people who dislike Irish say, "Well, I love Irish and it's very important, but it's of no practical value, for practical reasons we have to use English." You get this again and again – the word "practical" comes in both at the EU level and in Ireland. People say, "We have to use English, as everybody knows English," which is false. It is completely inaccurate to say that everybody speaks English, *they do not*. Over the past five years, my wife, being French here in Vienna, believed this propaganda in the beginning and tried to use English alone. She found that cashiers in supermarkets in Vienna mostly do not speak English. She repeatedly found that technicians coming to repair things at the house do not speak English. It was driven home to her from practical daily experience that not everybody speaks English, even in Austria. The level of English in Austria would be higher than, say, in more southern European countries or in Slavic countries, but even in Vienna it is impossible to use English alone for everyday life.

The limited use of English in Europe is the reality. If everybody spoke English, then there would be no need for interpretation and translation in the European Parliament – we could have debates in English alone, and voters would be obliged to elect people who speak fluent English. This would interfere with the democratic right of citizens to elect the politicians they want and shows that language is far more important than is sometimes believed.

[There are two aspects of this question that I wanted to come back to if you agree. First, there is a bit of an argument going on because English hasn't been appointed by any current members of the European Union and it's going to remain an official language, and whether other languages should become official languages as well and based on what criteria. Is it that each member state gets to appoint one language? Should there be a numeric criterion, for example, in which case Catalan would be a good contender? So, there's this aspect of the question that I'd like to know what you think of. And the second one has to do with what you mentioned, I think we weren't recording, I don't know if you want to go into this, but you mentioned this difference between regional and minority languages, which is something I didn't really look into. You said, well, for example Irish should be protected, perhaps more than Catalan because Irish is only spoken in Ireland by a few people, and it really is endangered, whereas Catalan is a Romance language which is very similar to Spanish, which has a large community. So maybe this need not have a one-size-fits-all solution, but we should rather look at particular regional and minority languages in specific contexts and say, "Okay, this needs more protection than that," you know?]

I'm glad you raised these points because there's a lot of misunderstanding about the official languages in the EU. The factual position is that as a new country joins the EU, that country's official language, or official languages, become official EU languages. That has been the position since the first regulation passed by the EU in 1958 and, as new countries have joined, we went from four official EU languages to 24. The decision by Cyprus not to seek EU status for one of its official languages, Turkish, was essentially political.

Irish is a special case. When Ireland joined the EU (EEC, as it then was) in 1973, Irish was, for the first time, an official language of a member state which did *not* become an official language of the European Union. It became what they call a "treaty language" – in other words, they translated only the EU treaties into Irish. At the time, the Irish delegation argued in favour of Irish becoming an official language, but not a working language. There was strong opposition to this from speakers of other languages such as Danish and Dutch, who feared that their languages too could become official but not working languages, and that perhaps only English, French and German would be working languages. In fact, in the Commission, the latter three languages are what are called "procedural languages," but this is based on a mere internal decision, which has to be renewed by each new Commission. Italy has never been happy with this decision.

Irish, on 1 January 2007, became an official working language of the EU, but it was given a temporary derogation because of a lack of translators and interpreters. It was not possible to translate everything into Irish right away. The derogation is to end on 31 December 2021. Regarding translation and interpretation, Irish will then be in the same position as the other official working languages.

One Polish MEP, Danuta Hübner, suggested that now that the UK has left the European Union, English should be dropped as an official language. That was a non-starter from the beginning because changing the official languages requires a unanimous decision by the Council of Ministers. Because of this, there is no possibility of removing English as an official EU language. If the Spanish government, for instance, proposed to add Catalan as one of the official working languages of the European Union, this would need the unanimous consent of all EU governments. Ireland received this in 2005. If one country had said no, Irish would never have achieved EU status. The final country to agree was Austria, whose agreement followed contact at head of government level, as noted earlier. At present Catalan, Galician and Basque from Spain have a particular status – they may be used at council meetings, but Spain is responsible for financing this. Only the official working languages are financed from the EU budget.

The numerical criterion is not relevant. Catalan speakers say, "We have more speakers than Danish," which is true. But the only way Catalan could become an official working language of the EU is that, first of all, it becomes an official working language in all of Spain, not just in Catalonia. That would constitute a massive political change in Spain, and it would have to pass that hurdle first.

[Which is the situation with Turkish in Cyprus because Turkish is an official language in Cyprus, but it's not an official EU language. There's this discussion – well, should it be included then because it is an official language in Cyprus?]

I used to cover Cyprus and Turkey at one stage at the Irish Foreign Ministry and had a lot of meetings with Turkish and Cypriot colleagues, hearing their very different points of view. I asked different Cypriot colleagues if they spoke Turkish. The answer was invariably, "No, absolutely not." On the one hand, the government of Cyprus is the internationally recognised government of the whole island, but in joining the EU, even though Turkish is an official language in Cyprus, it did not request official status for Turkish. When I worked in DGT, some of my colleagues had already started to learn Turkish, with the idea that Turkish would eventually become an EU language.

The second point you raised: I think that there is a real need to look at the degree of difference between a language and other languages. Irish is a Celtic language, thus is very different to English. For instance, there is no verb "to have," there are mutations at the beginning of words – mother is "*máthair*," my mother is "*mo mháthair*," pronounced /mo va:hir/. You have a whole host of linguistic features in Irish that do not exist in non-Celtic languages such as English or French.

Turning to Catalan, which I never studied: at the time of the failed independence referendum in 2017, I often listened to speeches in Catalan. I noticed that because I speak French and I have a good knowledge of Spanish, I can understand a lot of Catalan and, certainly, when I see written Catalan, I can understand most of it. But to come back to the numeric criterion, even though Catalan has millions of speakers, that is never decisive. If it were decisive, German would become the first language of the EU. It has far more native speakers than any other language in the EU – about 100 million speakers. As an Austrian colleague mentioned to me yesterday, German has some status in more member states than any other language.

I speak as a person who really likes the German language – I speak German as much as possible with native speakers. I had two meetings yesterday at the Austrian Foreign Ministry and the Austrian Ministry of Education, one meeting of 45 minutes and the other half an hour, both of them in German. It was only German – *nur auf Deutsch*. This is normal because we are in Austria, and it is normal for a diplomat stationed in Austria to use the language of the country concerned. We discussed this point and we agreed that an Austrian diplomat stationed in Spain, for instance, should use Spanish.

I remember once attending a meeting in Lima, Peru, and noticing that diplomats from non-Spanish speaking countries were speaking to each other in Spanish. I found this very positive. It shows how inaccurate the idea is that English is *the* international language. English is an ethnic language in very wide international use.

Commentary

Initially and at first sight, the coronavirus pandemic of 2020–2022 showed the EU in a not particularly flattering light. There was little coordination, and especially little *solidarity*, among the member states, which rushed to shut their borders and defend their individual interests irrespective of the "common good." At the time, Enrico Letta fittingly suggested that the "Trump virus" might turn out to be more lethal than COVID-19 – referring to Donald Trump's presidential campaign slogan of 2016, "America first." If every EU country put its interests first, they would "all sink together" (Letta, quoted in Rankin 2020). Yet health was not an EU area of competence and, even within nations as small as, for instance, Austria, there was a lot of disagreement among the *Bundesländer* [states] (see, e.g., Gebhart 2020). Thus, expecting instant consensus and full harmony among 27 member states seems unrealistic, especially when the EU had no mandate to act in this area.

In any case, once the initial shock waves of the pandemic subsided, the EU did reveal itself as a community of shared fate in formation. This took place both at the national level – with member states showing solidarity towards their neighbours by shouldering their hospital burden – *and* at the transnational level – with the EU arriving at an unprecedented, and until then unthinkable, consensus around contracting collective debt and allowing member states to pay back according to their individual financial possibilities.

In this chapter's interview, Ó Riain raises the controversial question of solidarity – what Jean Asselborn termed "solidarity crisis" [*Solidaritätskrise*] recently (Asselborn 2020). Ó Riain approaches it through the lens of European identity, a shared identity, as it were. But perhaps we ought to substitute this by the notion of shared fate, as noted in the introduction above. This shift moves the focus away from the slippery slope of ethnic or even linguistic identity to allow the more practical and immediate notion of shared fate to take centre stage. A community of (shared) fate does not require a common identity, nor is it structured around a common language.

Shared fate is grounded in parity of esteem (see Chapter 4), and parity of esteem is crucial in multilingual settings as regards not only language policy but also language practices. One of the questions discussed by Ó Riain in the interview above is that of the current number of official EU languages. He dismisses the numeric criterion, claiming that the corollary of this approach would be German becoming the bloc's lingua franca by the sheer force of the number of its native speakers. Yet the introduction of a lingua franca is off the table in any case. Moreover and more importantly, the custodians of multilingualism in the EU, the DGT, use the fact that English is the most widely spoken additional language in the EU as the semi-official reason behind the unofficial status of the language as the bloc's lingua franca (see Leal 2021, 207–214). If the EU were to finally address its language policies, practices and ideologies, as recommended within the three turns proposed here, clarifying the role of the numeric criterion in this context would be of paramount importance. Creating a pluricentric agency for language policy and planning should help in setting a direction in the EU's approach to granting official status to new languages.

In this context, Ó Riain also emphasises that the post-Brexit role of English shall *not* change, as adding or excluding a language would require consensus among all member states. More importantly, however, he stresses that there was never a rule whereby each acceding nation gets to appoint a single language to attain official EU status. Instead, all member states' national languages become official EU languages automatically. The thorny question of the lack of official status for Turkish, one of the two official languages in Cyprus, remains, nevertheless. Even though it would be hasty and simply inaccurate to say that English will or even should lose its EU status in the wake of Brexit – which Polish Member of the European Parliament Danuta Hübner actually suggested, as noted by Ó Riain – there does seem to be a double standard in the EU as regards the addition/exclusion of official languages – one that should at long last be addressed by the EU. It does not suffice to say that "the powers that be" in Cyprus are not interested in granting official status to Turkish, particularly when we have future accessions in mind. The linguistic landscape of most candidate states is intricate – let us think of Bosnia, for example, with its three official languages, namely Bosnian, Croatian and Serbian.

Another aspect surrounding the number of official EU languages addressed by Ó Riain in this chapter is that of differentiated protection for certain languages based on their "uniqueness" and level of endangerment. The latest edition of the *UNESCO Atlas of the World's Languages in Danger* (Moseley 2010) lists 2,500 languages, 109 of which are spoken in the EU – the majority of which are spoken in Italy (32) and France (26). Another three languages have become extinct in the EU since the 1950s according to the *Atlas*, namely Dalmatian in Croatia, Guanche in Spain and Slovincian in Poland. These two factors – i.e., how unique a language is in terms of its language family and how severely its vitality is under threat – should be considered by the EU if it were to take a more coherent stance in relation to language policy.

This notwithstanding, languages not currently under immediate threat and/or not in relative genealogical isolation should still be granted rights and protections – though perhaps of a different nature. The personal criterion should not be forgotten in this context, and the numeric criterion is difficult to ignore. Why should speakers of, say, Mirandés, an endangered language spoken by several thousands in north-eastern Portugal, be granted special rights and incentives while Basque, spoken by nearly 1 million in Spain and France, not be granted any? Because Mirandés is in a more vulnerable position and may become extinct before the end of this century. However, this is not at odds with the practical needs of those nearly 1 million Basque speakers, who cherish their language just as much as Mirandés speakers and need incentives and opportunities to use Basque in public life. We can concur with Ó Riain that different languages require a different set of measures – while

Mirandés may need urgent subsidies to foster its vitality, Basque may require inclusion in different areas of public life. It should not, however, be a question of fostering only those languages under immediate threat, as was the rationale behind the ECRML at its inception (see Chapter 1).

As underlined in the Introductory remarks, languages entail options and ligatures. Fostering ligatures by providing options associated with particular languages should be the priority of an EU-wide pluricentric agency for language policy and planning – thus creating options to gain access to education, jobs, public services, cultural goods, prestige and esteem. Creating options to foster ligatures does not necessarily entail adding official languages to the EU's 24, as already noted. However beneficial official EU status may be for the development and the prestige of a given language, this can be achieved through other – top-down and bottom-up – measures which engender incentives and opportunities to use this language, thus fostering its speakers' language ligatures. A pluricentric agency for language policy and planning could do precisely that, thus circumventing the thorny issue of official EU status (and the need for consensus) while offering speakers of non-EU languages the required protections.

Through this perspective, the question of whether there should be more official EU languages becomes more multifaceted, as official EU status is no longer perceived as the be-all end-all of EU language policy. Perhaps a gradual change in language ideologies in the EU, coupled with a shift towards more intercomprehension, would allow for more languages to be granted official EU status without placing too large a burden on the bloc's institutional set-up. Also, or alternatively, if Ó Riain's suggestion to introduce Esperanto as *de jure* and *de facto* lingua franca (into which documents are translated and oral input is interpreted) could be implemented, this would also allow for the number of official languages to increase more or less comfortably.

However, the bottom line seems to be rather *whether* and *how* the EU approaches its language issues than its *number* of official languages.[7] Measures such as that suggested by Ó Riain in the context of the Irish Parliament would go a long way to raise the status of speakers of a given language and, by extension, of the language as well. Once again, we see Van Parijs's "maxi-min principle" in action in the example discussed by Ó Riain above (Van Parijs

2011, 14 – see Chapters 3 and 4). Though Irish could be spoken more often in the Irish Parliament given the number of Irish-speaking members of parliament in the country, the maxi-min principle perpetuates the perceived need to speak English to maximise intelligibility, and thus political support. Introducing Irish-only times is a promising top-down measure to break this vicious circle – a measure which dovetails with the notion of "aimed equity" proposed in Chapter 4, whereby the EU should at least attempt to achieve a more balanced use of its official languages to counter the current 90–95 per cent dominance of English as a drafting language.

In the case both of the Irish Parliament and the EU, state interference in the form of top-down language policy is justified, as argued in Chapter 2. There is abundant scientific evidence that a *laissez-faire* approach in the realm of language is not beneficial if the intention is to protect languages and maintain (and/or foster) individual and state multilingualism (see, e.g., Grin 2006, 83–84; Johnson 2013, 23; Wickström et al. 2018). This notwithstanding, grassroots initiatives can also go a long way towards achieving the same goal and, ideally, both top-down and bottom-up levels should come together through piecemeal, multifaceted measures to engender and reflect renewed language ideologies in the bloc.

Notes

1 See www.unesco.org/languages-atlas, last accessed in December 2022.
2 Ó Riain complements this appraisal by reminding us that "[t]he principal voluntary language restoration movement, *Conradh na Gaeilge/* the Gaelic League, was founded on 31 July 1893, following Dr Douglas Hyde's seminal lecture 'On the Necessity for De-Anglicising Ireland' in November 1892. The *Conradh* is still active today" (private communications).
3 Though the controversial "Basic Law: Israel as the Nation-State of the Jewish People," from 2018, changes the status of Arabic from "official" to "special."
4 Ó Riain adds, however, that the "higher" and "lower" roles that comprise diglossia have a unique dynamic in Ireland, because Irish, albeit less widely spoken, enjoys more prestige than English, albeit dominant. In his words, "[t]he situation in Ireland is perhaps unique: though Irish offers incomparably fewer options than English, an added complication

since Irish independence in 1922 is the increasing links between Irish and level of education. In Ireland, the less educated all speak English; whereas among university graduates a far greater proportion are bilingual and speak Irish fluently. This gives a prestige to Irish which is difficult to reconcile with seeing it as 'lower'" (private communications).
5 Interestingly, Ó Riain reports that the final state to agree to official EU status for Irish in 2005 was Austria. The person in charge of this policy area had lived for just six months in Ireland to cover the Irish EU Presidency of 1990. As she was so busy, she did not travel much and experienced Ireland as Dublin only – the most anglicised part of Ireland. She hence concluded that it made no sense to grant official EU status to a language no one spoke in Ireland. She was eventually overruled politically when the Irish *Taoiseach*/Prime Minister contacted his Austrian counterpart (private communications).
6 According to Ó Riain, it was enacted in December 2021, and its practical benefits are already being felt – for instance, all public bodies are now required by law to produce 20 per cent of their communications – whether written or electronic – with the public in Irish (private communications).
7 Ó Riain adds that he once attended an all-day Council of the EU meeting on multilingualism where ministers from all 28 member states spoke (it was before Brexit). The vast majority of ministers spoke in support of multilingualism, and of national and EU action to strengthen it. There were two exceptions, namely the UK and the Netherlands. The latter two ministers opposed any state or EU intervention in the language area and supported a *laissez-faire* approach – "give everybody freedom to use whatever language they wish," as they put it. Ó Riain comments further that the French writer Henri Lacordaire once put it, "*entre le fort et le faible, c'est la liberté qui opprime et la loi qui affranchit*" [between the strong and the weak, it is freedom that oppresses and the law that frees] (private communications).

References

Arzoz (ed.), Xabier. 2008. *Respecting linguistic diversity in the European Union*. Amsterdam & Philadelphia: John Benjamins.

Asselborn, Jean, interview by Ingrid Steiner-Gashi. 2020. "'Grenzschutz-Fetischismus'." *Kurier*. (22 April).

Balibar, Étienne. 2014. *Equaliberty: Political essays*. Translated by James Ingram. Durham & London: Duke University Press.

Fishman, Joshua A. 1967. "Bilingualism with and without diglossia; diglossia with and without bilingualism." *Journal of Social Issues* XXIII (2): 29–38.

Gazzola, Michele. 2014. *Partecipazione, esclusione linguistica e traduzione: Una valutazione del regime linguistico dell'Unione Europea*. *Studi Italiani di Linguistica Teorica e Applicata*, XLIII (2): 227–264.
Gazzola, Michele, and François Grin. 2013. "Is ELF more effective and fair than translation? An evaluation of the EU's multilingual regime." *International Journal of Applied Linguistics* 23 (1): 93–107.
Gebhart, Martin. 2020. "Ein neuer Föderalismus muss her." *Kurier*, 28 April: 2.
Grin, François. 2006. "Economic considerations in language policy." In *An introduction to language policy: Theory and method*, edited by Thomas Ricento, 75–94. Malden: Blackwell Publishing.
Johnson, David Cassels. 2013. *Language policy*. London: Palgrave Macmillan.
Kraus, Peter A. 2008. *A union of diversity: Language, identity and polity-building in Europe*. Cambridge: Cambridge University Press.
Kraus, Peter A. 2018. "From glossophagic hegemony to multilingual pluralism?: Re-assessing the politics of linguistic identity in Europe." In *The politics of multilingualism: Europeanisation, globalisation and linguistic governance*, edited by François Grin and Peter A. Kraus, 89–109. Amsterdam & Philadelphia: John Benjamins.
Leal, Alice. 2021. *English and translation in the European Union: Unity and multiplicity in the wake of Brexit*. Abingdon & New York: Routledge.
Leal, Alice. 2022. "The European Union's translation policies, practices and ideologies: Time for a translation turn." *Perspectives: Studies in Translation Theory and Practice* 30 (2): 195–208.
Leal, Alice. 2023. "Towards a multilingual modus operandi in the EU." *Just. Journal of Language Rights & Minorities, Revista de Drets Lingüístics i Minories* 2 (1) 149–176.
Mercator European Research Centre on Multilingualism and Language Learning. 2016. *The Irish language in education in the Republic of Ireland*. Ljouwert: Mercator.
Mintel, Julina, and Nicolai von Ondarza. 2022. "More EU decisions by qualified majority voting – but how?" *Stiftung Wissenschaft und Politik*, 19 10: 1–8. doi:10.18449/2022C61.
Moseley, Chistopher. (Ed.). 2010. *Atlas of the world's languages in danger*. Paris: UNESCO Publishing.
Phillipson, Robert. 2003. *English-only Europe?: Challenging language policy*. London & New York: Routledge.
Shohamy, Elana. 2006. *Language policy: Hidden agendas and new approaches*. Abingdon & New York: Routledge.
Spolsky, Bernard. 2004. *Language policy*. Cambridge: Cambridge University Press.

van Gunsteren, Herman R. 2018. *A theory of citizenship: Organizing plurality in contemporary democracies.* Abingdon & New York: Routledge.

Van Parijs, Philippe. 2011. *Linguistic justice for Europe and for the world.* Oxford: Oxford University Press.

Wickström, Bengt-Arne, Michele Gazzola, and Torsten Templin. 2018. "Can the 'free market' manage language diversity?" In *Mobility and inclusion in multilingual Europe: The MIME Vademecum*, edited by François Grin, 34–35.

Williams, Melissa S. 2004. "Sharing the river: Aboriginal representation in Canadian political institutions." In *Representation and democratic theory*, edited by David Laycock, 93–118. Vancouver & Toronto: UBC Press.

6 Ireland and multilingualism in a post-Brexit EU

Introductory remarks

In 2021, Ó Riain was appointed Multilingualism Officer by the Irish Department of Foreign Affairs – a post that has no counterpart in the other EU member states, at least not to our knowledge. This post is relevant for two main clusters of reasons. First, because it encapsulates the shift in the EU's linguistic landscape brought about by Brexit. Ireland's reaction to Brexit – as the only EU member state where English is the main language – will set the tone of future discussions on the role of English and multilingualism in the bloc. Second, because this new assignment is an innovative, bold step towards strengthening multilingualism in Ireland, and lessons learned from this experience can be valuable to all member states. This chapter features a discussion of how Ó Riain's new post came into being against the backdrop of the UK's withdrawal from the EU; a suggestion of the main tasks and challenges it entails; as well as a presentation of strategies to deal with these challenges – which can be extrapolated beyond the Irish diplomatic service.

Regarding the future of English in the EU, as noted in the previous chapter, its official status will remain unchanged, as any language additions or exclusions require unanimity among all member states. Ó Riain believes, however, that English will gradually lose importance in the bloc as fewer and fewer British citizens work at EU institutions, bodies and agencies, and as the demographic strength of native speakers of the language falls dramatically to just about 1 per cent of the EU's population. In his view, these factors explain Ireland's precautionary measures

DOI: 10.4324/9781003342069-6

to engender a gradual shift towards a more multilingual *modus operandi* as opposed to the current largely monolingual anglophone approach – at least in its diplomatic service which, albeit restricted, is telling of the country's general direction regarding multilingualism.

British citizens currently working at EU institutions, bodies and agencies may stay until retirement, as pointed out by Ó Riain in what follows. Nevertheless, they may be restricted in what they actually can do given that their country is no longer a part of the club. It is certainly not a case of the British "los[ing] their jobs" in the EU, as hastily suggested by Marko Modiano (2017, 315). However, British citizens are no longer hired by the EU, which means that the next few decades will witness a sharp decline in the number of EU internal staff from the UK. Anglophones have been known to dominate in various EU key areas – 42 per cent of the EU commissioners' spokespersons, for instance, were native speakers of English in 2010, as noted in Chapter 4 (Grin 2015, 134–135 – see Leal 2021, 149). Therefore, perhaps Ó Riain is right to forecast a decline in the language's profile in the EU.

However, we should bear in mind that the EU can still outsource certain tasks and hire external staff from the UK, which is relevant particularly in the context of the EU's language services (as reported by Jeremy Gardner, former senior translator at the Court of Auditors of the EU – see Leal 2021, 172). A rough estimate of the number of internal translators, interpreters and other language experts currently employed in EU bodies, agencies and institutions surpasses 5,000, and the number of freelancers used annually is probably just as high. This is nearly 10 per cent of the EU's total internal staff, so these numbers are significant (Leal 2021, 90–91). It does not look like English will lose influence in the language services – and hence in the institutions, bodies and agencies as a whole – due to a lack of native speakers, given that this will probably be compensated for by external staff.

These facts are also relevant in conjunction with the possibility of the establishment of a variety of English that is exclusive to the EU – an issue raised and dismissed by Ó Riain in what follows. As noted in Chapter 3, different schools of thought perceive this matter differently. The World Englishes paradigm, spearheaded, for example, by Modiano, maintains that the distance from the UK brought about by Brexit will provide fertile ground for the development of a "quasi-Outer Circle" variety of English, "not decidedly based on any one Inner Circle variety but (...) characterized by influences from standardized English as well as their [speakers'] native tongues" and by "culture-specific features common to the manner in which English is used as an L2 in continental Europe" (Modiano 2017, 313, 322). Yet somewhat contradictorily, he also predicts that what he calls "Euro-English" will follow American English – an issue to which we will come back below.

Diarmait Mac Giolla Chríost and Matteo Bonotti concur with Modiano in that they see Brexit as an opportunity to detach the English language from Britain, thus making it "neutral" and "Esperantized": "Since English, after Brexit, would no longer be associated with the collective identity of any linguistic community within the EU (...), there would no longer be the need to ensure parity of esteem between English and other languages" (Mac Giolla Chríost and Bonotti 2018, 68). They call this new variety EGLF, i.e., English as a global lingua franca.

The English as a lingua franca (ELF) paradigm holds a similar view, though they insist on the fluidity and hybridity of ELF and thus refrain from claiming variety status. Alessia Cogo and Jennifer Jenkins (2010), for example, propose a revision of the EU's notions of language and multilingualism to accommodate this fluidity, along with the adoption of "European ELF" as its *exclusive* lingua franca – a suggestion also made by Modiano, Mac Giolla Chríost and Bonotti, the difference in terminology notwithstanding. Yet none of them seem to account for the two key facts outlined earlier, namely (1) that the British will not disappear from EU institutions, bodies and agencies and, even if they did, (2) a lot of the influence and prestige associated with the English language comes from the USA, due primarily to everyone's exposure to (audio, visual and audio-visual) material from the country. This remains unaltered by Brexit, so it may be premature to speak of a detachment from inner-circle English(es) in the EU.

On the other hand, there is the question of a lack of prestige or perhaps even a certain resentment towards the UK and, by extension, the English language, in the aftermath of Brexit. Jean-Claude Juncker, president of the European Commission at the time of the Brexit vote, confirmed on at least two occasions that "slowly but surely English is losing importance in Europe" (May 2016) and that "we are not under the rule of the only lingua franca, which is English" (September 2018) (Stolton 2018). We could attribute these remarks to his unmistakable sense of humour, but there was a noticeable increase in the use of French and German in speeches and statements to the press after the Brexit referendum, a shift confirmed by some of my interviewees in the EU in 2020 (Leal 2021 – see, e.g., Steinhauser 2016; Derlén 2018, 347).

Those readers residing in the EU will have anecdotal evidence of the bitter taste that Brexit has left in everyone's mouths, gradually changing the way the EU perceives the UK. The political turmoil that ensued in the UK only intensified these negative sentiments towards everything British. It is no coincidence that anti-EU movements across the bloc have either slowed down or come to a complete halt in the aftermath of Brexit, as revealed in a 2022 survey conducted by the European Social Survey (Henley 2023). More research is needed to ascertain whether and to what extent these factors have an impact on European's desire and willingness to speak or learn English. The facts remain that, on the one hand, a nation's prestige impacts its language(s) profile on the global stage (see Ostler 2010) while, on the other, the influence of the USA remains untouched by Brexit. Let us keep this background information in mind as we move on to the interview.

Interview

13 *You have recently been appointed Multilingualism Officer by the Irish government, a newly created post based in Brussels. What does this role entail and what are your plans for it?*
A. I have been appointed Multilingualism Officer by the Irish Department of Foreign Affairs. The Secretary General/SG said that a problem in the Irish diplomatic service is that it is too monolingual. Most colleagues are only comfortable working in English. They might have learned some French, Spanish or German but not enough to be comfortable working in those languages.

Following Brexit, Ireland is the only country in the EU where the vast majority of the population are native English speakers, which means that, in 27 EU countries, only about 1 per cent of the overall population are native speakers of English. In this situation, the SG felt we need to do something about increasing both the study and, more importantly, the regular use of other languages.

Thus, he has created this position for me. He said he noticed that not only do I speak far more languages than most of my colleagues, but that I seem to have a passion for language and language policy like nobody else in our service. He asked me if I would accept this challenge; he is conscious of how difficult it is, because most colleagues are in a rather comfortable situation. They are working in a world where all diplomats now speak fluent English. This means that Irish diplomats are going against the grain if they wish to use another language. The easy thing to do is to continue working in English and let the others make the effort. This looks *prima facie* like a good idea.

When one goes deeper, of course, it becomes apparent that it is not a good idea. Imagine, for instance, that German were to have the position in the EU that English currently occupies. Then all Irish diplomats would have not only to master their specialisation, but also master German in order to express themselves. However, they would be interacting daily with native speakers of German, who have mastered the language thoroughly through lifelong use. How would my Irish colleagues feel in that situation? It is part of my job to bring home to people how unfair and unjust the present situation is.

Some people cannot imagine a situation being radically different from what it is today. English is at present the most widely used international language. They forget that language use can be subject to governmental decisions. In our own constitution, for instance, Article 8 says that Irish is the first official language. English is recognised as a second official language, but there's a third part which says that nothing in this constitution will prevent the parliament from legislating for the exclusive use of either of the two languages – in either part or the whole of the national territory. Such legislation has never been passed. I think the reason may have been to show, even if there were a reunification of Ireland, that there would never be an imposition of Irish on Northern Ireland. It shows that the framers of the constitution appreciated that government decisions can influence the use of language.

When I was in Poland, for instance, in the 90s, preparing for EU entry, the mysterious decision was taken that the Polish side had to present all papers for discussion to the EU in English. They had to have them translated from Polish at their own expense. They were not given the opportunity of presenting them in English, French or German; Poland was compelled to use English and nothing else.

Who decided this and where remains anonymous, but the decision was strictly enforced.

To come back to the new post, as I understand it, my main duty will be to increase the motivation of colleagues to learn and use other languages, to move away from the English monolingual *ethos*, which has been dominant for so long. It is an extremely difficult task, due to the present ubiquity of English in diplomacy. I will have to look at best practice in many other countries, particularly English-speaking countries.

For instance, when I served in Australia in 1990, the Australian Foreign Ministry paid its diplomats 600 dollars a year extra for every Western European language they mastered, 1,200 dollars a year for every Slavic language they mastered, and 2,400 dollars a year for what they considered very difficult language, like Mandarin Chinese, Vietnamese, Arabic. To earn this language allowance, you had to do a difficult exam every two years to prove that you had not lost fluency in the language. There was no limit to the number of languages you could do, as long as they were useful to the Australian foreign service. This Australian system continues today. The US and the UK run similar systems.

At the time, I sent all the details back to Dublin – of course, nothing happened, they were set in their old monolingual groove in Dublin in 1990. But now, 30 years later, being in a position of being just 1 per cent native English speakers in the EU, the situation has changed radically. In order to deepen our relations with other countries, such as our economic relations with France and Germany, we need diplomats who are fluent in French, German and other languages.

The Irish diplomatic service has decided already on its six key languages: all the UN languages, except English and Russian. This means French, Spanish, Chinese and Arabic, and they have added Portuguese and German. Two of them, Mandarin Chinese and Arabic, are considered very difficult. It would take most people two years studying full time to be able to work comfortably in them.

So, my job would basically be to increase motivation, to get people to use the amount of other languages they already know, and by doing so to learn more. Somebody who knows some French, for instance, and is sitting beside a French or Belgian colleague in Brussels, but they normally speak only English. They could suggest speaking French over a coffee. Things as simple as that.

When I worked in the permanent representation in Brussels in 2005–2007, I organised an Irish-language coffee morning every Friday. About a dozen of us would get together in Rue Froissart and speak Irish over coffee. This worked well and could be used for any language, such as a French-speaking coffee. I was a member of a polyglot club in Brussels, where they had flags on different tables representing different languages. So, you could decide which language you wished to practise and go to the appropriate table. Online discussion groups considerably increase the potential.

In Ireland we have had an Irish language policy for a century, where they've been teaching the language and where people are examined regularly to see what level they've reached. However, they never connected this with the actual use of the language, and there seems to be a failure to understand that you need to use a language to improve. Learning languages that you have no opportunity to use is like trying to fill a bathtub with no stopper in it. There is a huge amount of learning, but fluency is never reached.

This is one of my tasks to get across to colleagues: that in order to improve, they need to start using their languages, now, right away, tomorrow. There is a false idea that they need to keep learning until they become fluent speakers first of all, and then someday they'll magically decide, "Now I know the language, now I can start speaking it perfectly." It does not work like that. One learns by making mistakes and it can be an amusing process. For instance, when I served in Vienna in the 1980s, an Irish senator, Micheál Yeats, came here. His wife, Gráinne Yeats, was a well-known harpist, and she was attending an international gathering of harpists. Both are fluent Irish speakers. I had lunch with them a few times. Senator Micheál Yeats was the son of the poet W. B. Yeats, a Nobel prize winner, and he told me that his father had wanted to learn to speak Irish all his life, but he wanted to speak it faultlessly. He learned reams of poetry by heart, and 20 pages of prose, and he could recite both. However, he never learned to speak the language because of this fear of making mistakes. One of my main tasks will be to try to weaken this false belief that you need to become perfect in the language before you start speaking it. I need to get across to my colleagues that making mistakes is a necessary part of learning a language. They will improve by practising what they already know, for real communication.

When I arrived in Poland, I had only had two classes of Polish, so I knew almost nothing. I took intensive courses for the first three months, and then decided that I needed to practise what I was learning. So I asked the local staff at our embassy in Warsaw to speak Polish to me, all the time. This gave me two difficult months. I made all kinds of funny mistakes in Polish, but we stuck to it. My Polish started to improve, from using it day in, day out, making mistakes and then correcting the mistakes.

I remember on one occasion a rather amusing mistake: we were tired after a day's work but decided to have a coffee and a chat before going home. We were talking about children – I wanted to say that my sister had twins four years previously, so I composed the sentence in my mind, but I got one word wrong. The Polish word for twins is *"bliźniaki,"* and for some reason I said *"ziemniaki."* So what I really said was, "Four years ago, my sister had potatoes." This brought down the house in laughter, and I laughed along with them. They never forgot this and for years afterwards, they would ask me, "How are the *ziemniaki* (potatoes) getting on?"

I will have to be quite creative in this role, to come up with new ideas and added value. The importance of languages and language policy tends to be underestimated all the time, so one of my own tasks will be to push this item up the policy agenda, to show colleagues that it is more important than they realise. This could add to the motivation to study and use other languages. If colleagues see languages as just being a neutral instrument, and that different languages are just different ways of saying the same thing, then they will be less motivated to learn. If you already have the best neutral instrument, why waste time looking for neutral instruments that are less widely used in the world? My core task will be to show that language is more than a neutral instrument.

There are important factors that are not well known: Professor François Grin prepared a report for the French government in 2005 showing that the international dominance of the English language brings between €17 and 18 billion to the UK economy every year. This is three times as much as North Sea oil. This 130-page report is available in French on the internet, and it shows precisely how this figure was calculated. It includes the hundreds of thousands of people going to Britain to study English each year, the vast production of material for the worldwide study of English, etc. In comparison, few people go to Poland just to learn Polish.

I would like to survey colleagues on frequency of use of their languages – under each language, do they use it daily, weekly, once a month, occasionally or never? This is quite new in the Irish census now – for a long time, it asked, "Do you speak Irish only, English only or both languages?" and now it asks, "How often do you speak Irish?" Daily, weekly, monthly, occasionally. We have figures now for those who speak it – we know that something like 74,000 people, outside of the educational system, speak Irish every day. It's about 2 per cent of the population – more than three-quarters live in Dublin and in cities outside the traditional Irish-speaking areas. Most books in Irish are bought in the Dublin area, which a century ago was the most anglicised part of Ireland. Then I would like to contact the foreign ministries of different countries and check the incentives that they use. I have already spoken to my Belgian, Danish, Norwegian, Australian and Canadian colleagues about this.

14 *To my knowledge, your new post has no counterpart in other EU countries. As noted earlier, the EU itself has no portfolio or unit dedicated to multilingualism. What do you think motivated Ireland to take this step? Do you think other member states might follow suit?*
A. First of all, one of the reasons Ireland is taking this step now is Brexit. They have realised that native English speakers are just 1 per cent of the population of the 27 EU countries. There is a feeling that English is in a very privileged position as the most used language in the EU institutions. The more thoughtful colleagues are beginning to wonder if this can last. It will not change quickly. English, of course, will retain its status as one of the official working languages of the EU, but the EU will not be recruiting new people from the UK from now on. Permanent UK officials may stay until retirement if they wish. But because their country is no longer a member state, they are likely to be less involved in more important decisions. Ireland joined *La Francophonie* in October 2018, and the Brexit referendum was in June 2016. The Secretary General who made this decision announced a few days ago that he has become Irish ambassador to France. And it was also announced that we are now opening a new consulate general in Lyon as well, to deepen our economic relationship with France.

I have not discussed this very much with my EU colleagues yet, just with my Belgian colleague, who represents her country at the IAEA. She told me that she felt this was a good idea and that it would be worth copying in other countries. It is something I will discuss with different colleagues from now on. I have also arranged to meet the representative of *La Francophonie* in Brussels.

The EU decision to drop a unit dedicated to multilingualism was a move in the wrong direction, and its decision-makers need to revise this. They need to read the academic literature in this area; I would mention, for instance, *English-only Europe?* by Professor Robert Phillipson, published in 2003, and *Linguistic Imperialism* and a whole host of books about the dominance of English in Europe. Professor Phillipson told me that, in 15 years, his book *English-only Europe?* had only sold about 2,000 copies, which is tiny in an EU of 450 million people. Many decision-makers have never read this book and may not even be aware of it. This is a crucial problem. One of my tasks would be to try to get across this idea that if you are working in an area, you at least need to study the academic work that has been done. It is time to recognise that, in this area, the EU has been going in the wrong direction for the last 15 years.

We need to recognise that there is a problem, that English isn't just a neutral instrument, but a language rooted in UK, American, Australian history, etc. Any idea of Euro-English is a non-starter, in my view. Over 43 years of experience in diplomacy has shown me that such an idea will never be taken seriously. If Europe tried to develop its own English, it would be regarded internationally as poorly learned English. If somebody contends that ELF [English as a lingua franca] exists as a serious category, ask them for a list of publications in this new variety of English!

This whole idea of ELF: I am afraid I strongly disagree with any English as a lingua franca as being distinct from the English of the English-speaking countries, particularly the US. It would never be taken seriously by the Americans and others who speak the language natively. The sooner this idea is dropped, the sooner we get back to real consideration of language policy – looking at alternatives which do exist, looking at intercomprehension, for instance, between language families and a whole host of areas that have been ignored. Far too many resources have been put into this ELF area. It is time to correct the mistakes.

15 *So you feel that your new post is a direct consequence of Brexit?*
A. There was probably no conscious decision taken, but I think the chronology speaks for itself. French has been the main foreign

Ireland and multilingualism in a post-Brexit EU 139

language taught in Irish schools for centuries, and we have been independent for the last century, since 1922. I think there was a general move towards – possibly as a psychological reaction to Brexit – strengthening our links with continental countries. For instance, beyond the linguistic area, the number of direct sea links between Ireland and France has increased from 12 to 44 since Brexit. We have had more sailings, such as more boat links between Cork and Spain. In addition, we have had a programme of ministerial visits to all EU countries, including countries with whom we have not had, historically, very close links.

There is a general trend, broader than the impact of Brexit, but strengthened by it. Our links have been strengthened in the past number of years since EU enlargement, for instance, we have had a lot of immigration. We have 136,000 people in Ireland speaking Polish at home now, and their children have excellent pronunciation in Irish in school. Increasing numbers of Lithuanians, Latvians, Slovaks, Romanians, Central and Eastern Europeans have made Ireland their home. When the EU enlarged in 2004, we opened our doors to permit people from any EU country to work in Ireland. Not all EU countries were as open. Quite a large number of people moved to Ireland at that stage, so we suddenly heard a lot of different languages. It was, in a sense, a move away from the old monolingual English-speaking island, a product of the nineteenth century.

The very fact that there are more people speaking different languages in Ireland also encourages the use of Irish. An organisation called "iMeasc," meaning "integrate," was set up in 2006 for recent immigrants to Ireland who had learned to speak Irish well, and to promote the Irish language among immigrants. One of the members of "iMeasc," the Dutchman Alex Hijmans, has written novels in Irish and now lives in Brazil, where he continues to write regularly in Irish. On one occasion I heard a radio programme, which shows how far the colonisation has gone in the Irish psyche. There was a programme in English on the radio about iMeasc, and somebody phoned in with a strong Dublin accent and said, "You don't understand our culture; we hate Irish." This guy would have seen himself as Irish, but an Irish person who hated his own roots, who hated the language which gave meaning to his own surname, which gave meaning to the name of his own city. Dublin is just "*Dubhlinn*," from "*Dubh*," meaning "black" and "*linn*," "a pool."

By knowing Irish, the place names of the whole island of Ireland, and of most of Scotland, begin to make sense. A whole tradition becomes a closed book if you ignore the language – this provided an extra reason for devoting some attention to Irish.

To come back to Brexit. Just yesterday the government decided to set up an Irish consulate general in Lyon to strengthen economic links with France. We are returning to our roots because some 15 centuries ago, the Irish were very involved on the Continent, spreading Christianity. Irish monks set up the *Schottenstift* in Vienna in 1155. *Scotus* in Latin meant an Irish speaker; Ireland in those days was called *Scotia Major*, and Scotland was *Scotia Minor* – when I joined the Foreign Ministry, we were shown a historical film called *When the Irish were Scots*. The Irish missionaries went as far as Kyiv. Saint Gall emigrated from Ireland in the year 613 AD and Christianised the area in Switzerland now called Sankt Gallen. And Columbanus went as far as northern Italy, to Bobbio.

Now we are going right back to this – restoring our ancient connection to continental Europe. Ireland has always been conscious of being a European country, and for centuries, when Catholicism was forbidden in Ireland, there were 18 Irish seminaries in France, many in Spain, and in what is now Belgium, then the Spanish Netherlands. Between 1600 and 1800, some 11,000 Irish priests were trained in France and smuggled back to Ireland in large boxes labelled *"oies sauvages,"* which gives us the origin of the Irish pub called *The Wild Geese* in Brussels.

Commentary

In this chapter's interview, Ó Riain indirectly approaches both linguistic justice and the notion of language options and ligatures, discussed in previous chapters. In his view, the most important task entailed in his post as Multilingualism Officer is to raise awareness – primarily among Irish diplomats but also beyond, as he is strategically based in Brussels – of the injustices that result from the dominance of English. He ties the need for a heightened awareness of these injustices to the need to foster ligatures to languages while also creating "incentives and opportunities" (Hornberger 2006, 32) to use these languages.

Yet all the while Ó Riain emphasises the importance of the economy as well, underlining the fact that these realms – i.e., that of language and that of the economy – go hand in hand. So "deepen[ing] ties with other nations" (Ó Riain in this chapter) involves upping diplomatic efforts – such as opening new consulates – strengthening political ties – through, for instance, ministerial visits – opening new sea links *and also* learning these nations' languages and fostering the linguistic and cultural realm – by joining *La Francophonie*, for example, and creating Ó Riain's post. The fact that the former secretary general of the Irish Department of Foreign Affairs took the decision to join *La Francophonie* and became Ambassador to France is no coincidence.

Raising awareness of linguistic (in)justice dovetails with the renewed role of language fostered within the language turn proposed here. Currently, an instrumental notion of language predominates among EU decision and policy-makers – as confirmed by Ó Riain and my own interviews in the EU (Leal 2021). Understanding that languages amount to more than mere vehicles that convey the same meanings in different ways – a very Platonic, outdated notion of language (Leal 2019) – is one of the core elements of the language turn and of Ó Riain's new post. This heightened awareness of the role of language as an important element in our identity layers means that there cannot be a no-policy language policy, which is another element Ó Riain is trying to impart on his peers. As suggested by Will Kymlicka (see De Schutter & Robichaud 2015, 89; Kraus 2008, 84), we can remove, say, religious symbols from public spaces, but we cannot remove language. Language is ubiquitous – regardless of whether we decide to speak about language policy, decisions about which language(s) (not) to use are made all the time. And this cannot be avoided.

Specifically regarding options and ligatures, the example of Irish education language policy Ó Riain discusses in this chapter epitomises the issue of a loss of ligatures due to a lack of options. Even though Irish has been taught in schools for a long time, this has not translated into a significant increase in the regular use of Irish. Without "incentives and opportunities" (Hornberger 2006, 32) to use the language beyond the education system, it is unlikely that ligatures to Irish will increase to the extent that it becomes, once again, a home language in many households. Irish started being taught thanks to both bottom-up and top-down language policies, but no significant financial measures were adopted to foster the economy of the *Gaeltacht*, the traditionally Irish-speaking areas of the country, leading to heavy emigration flows of Irish speakers to English-speaking countries.[1] When the policy was at long last expanded to encompass economic planning, those emigrants and their families did return to Ireland, but mainly as English speakers (see Spolsky 2004, 191; Leal 2021, 66–67).

There is a lot of scholarly debate about whether the comparison between the Irish language and the revitalisation of Hebrew in Israel is relevant and productive. Yet it is an undisputed fact that home language choice is pivotal when it comes to revitalisation, and one can only influence that decision when there are enough ligatures to the language in question, coupled with cherished, valuable and interesting options to use the language beyond the home and the school (see Spolsky 1991, 139 and 2004, 191–193; Leal 2021, 141).

Ó Riain also mentions the importance of conducting periodic, more detailed surveys of language *use* – rather than language *competence*, fraught as it is with the issues of self-assessment and the potential gap between competence and use. Traditional censuses often rely on an outdated notion of language as a static, monolithic unit "acquired" by a "speaker," who may or may not then go on to "acquire" additional languages in chronological order. As a result, these traditional surveys also rely on outdated methods to collect data on language practices and ideologies as they are, essentially, asking the wrong questions.

To my knowledge, the last comprehensive survey conducted by the EU in this realm took place in 2012, which in and of itself is telling of the lack of importance attributed to language policies, practices and ideologies by the EU (see European Commission 2012). The survey maps language proficiency in the bloc by following a strictly "mother tongue" and "additional," "other" or "foreign languages" approach, without accounting for individual multilingualism as the non-linear, non-chronological phenomenon that it is. Intercomprehension, language practices and language ideologies are barely touched upon. The survey's approach to language learning is also very much pre-"liberation linguistics," encapsulating the view outlined by Ó Riain in this chapter that one chooses a "foreign" language and then sits down and learns it "fully." On a positive note, however, the survey does inquire into attitudes towards translation, which is rare among censuses of this sort and a welcome development.

It is relevant that Ó Riain mentions the need for surveys that reflect language as the dynamic, multifaceted phenomenon that it is, and that doing precisely this is a part of his new post. At the national level, Bolivia probably has the most acclaimed census as regards thoroughness, dynamism and richness of detail. Though conducted only every ten years since 1992, it provides an impressive map of the country's linguistic landscape, accounting for language contact and individual multilingualism, while also taking stock of language practices and ideologies. Moreover, the results of the census feed directly into language policy and planning, as the country strives to maintain and foster the dozens of languages – particularly indigenous languages – spoken in its territory.

Contemporary language policy research offers innovative, interesting new methods to collect information on language (see, e.g., Baker 2006, 211, 216; Johnson 2013, especially his Chapters 5 and 6; Leal 2021, 72–73). As noted in previous chapters and mentioned by Ó Riain in this chapter, bridging the gap between academia and decision and policy-makers is an urgent matter, particularly in the realm of language and culture. For Ó Riain, this also poses a challenge for his new post, as he seeks to replace common-sense notions of and grave misconceptions about language. One way to achieve this is to create more opportunities for diplomats, policy and decision-makers to come together in dialogue with scholars through, for example, colloquia and workshops – a strategy Ó Riain intends to test.

This final interview ends with a thought-provoking parallel between present and past. Ó Riain speaks of a reconnecting with continental Europe through diplomatic, political and economic efforts, but also through linguistic and cultural initiatives – not merely as a gesture of goodwill, but as a genuine attempt to replace Ireland's current monolingual *modus operandi* through a multilingual mindset. As Paul Kaye, former language officer at the now defunct European Commission Representation in the UK, reminds us in an interview I conducted in 2020 (Leal 2021, 148), there is another side to the dominance of English and the injustices it creates. Growing up as an English native speaker has a "more subtle and insidious disadvantage," he notes, as one is not "forced into having to think in another language, into having to communicate in another language." On his account, this leads to an absence of "all the skills" associated with multilingualism, of "the insights into other cultures, into other ways of expressing yourself," of "that mental flexibility of slipping into and out of different languages." Overcoming this seems to be one of Ó Riain's main goals and, taken against the backdrop of Brexit, this also means distancing Ireland from the UK as regards its attitudes towards language and multilingualism.

Note

1 Ó Riain comments here that this policy can only be perceived as top-down since 1922, since "before that almost all primary schools were already teaching Irish, as there was a lot of popular pressure in favour of Irish before political independence." He adds that "on 9 September 1909, over 100,000 thronged the streets of Dublin demanding that matriculation in Irish be an essential condition for all students of the newly founded National University of Ireland." As a result, the university "yielded to popular pressure" and "from 1913, matriculation in Irish became a condition for all Irish-born students to study at the National University." This, in turn, "increased the percentage of primary schools offering Irish from 20 to close to 100 per cent," as support for Irish had been in sharp decline (private communications).

References

Baker, Colin. 2006. "Psycho-sociological analysis in language policy." In *An introduction to language policy: Theory and method*, edited by Thomas Ricento, 210–228. Malden: Blackwell Publishing.

De Schutter, Helder, and David Robichaud. 2015. "Van Parijsian linguistic justice – context, analysis and critiques." *Critical Review of International Social and Political Philosophy* 18 (2): 87–112.

Derlén, Mattias. 2018. "Multilingualism and the European Court of Justice: Challenges, reforms and the position of English after Brexit." In *The new EU judiciary. An analysis of current judicial reforms*, 341–356. Alphen aan den Rijn: Kluwer Law International.

European Commission. 2012. "Special Eurobarometer 386: Europeans and their languages." https://ec.europa.eu/commfrontoffice/publicopinion/archives/ebs/ebs_386_en.pdf.

Grin, François. 2015. "The economics of English in Europe." In *Language policy and political economy: English in a global context*, edited by Thomas Ricento, 119–144. Oxford: Oxford University Press.

Henley, Jon. 2023. "Support for leaving EU has fallen significantly across bloc since Brexit." *The Guardian*, 12 January.

Hornberger, Nancy H. 2006. "Frameworks and models in language policy and planning." In *An introduction to language policy: Theory and method*, edited by Thomas Ricento, 24–41. Malden: Blachwell Publishing.

Jenkins, Jennifer, and Alessia Cogo. 2010. "English as a lingua franca in Europe: A mismatch between policy and practice." *European journal of language policy* 2 (2): 271–294.

Johnson, David Cassels. 2013. *Language policy*. London: Palgrave Macmillan.

Kraus, Peter A. 2008. *A union of diversity: Language, identity and polity-building in Europe*. Cambridge: Cambridge University Press.

Kymlicka, Will. 1995. *Multicultural citizenship: A liberal theory of minority rights*. Oxford: Oxford University Press.

Leal, Alice. 2019. "Equivalence." In *The Routledge handbook of translation and philosophy*, edited by Piers Rawling and Philip Wilson, 224–242. Abingdon & New York: Routledge.

Leal, Alice. 2021. *English and translation in the European Union: Unity and multiplicity in the wake of Brexit*. Abingdon & New York: Routledge.

Mac Giolla Chríost, Diarmait, and Matteo Bonotti. 2018. *Brexit, language policy and linguistic diversity*. UK: Palgrave Macmillan.

Modiano, Marko. 2017. "English in a post-Brexit European Union." *World Englishes* 36 (3): 313–327.

Ostler, Nicholas. 2010. *The last lingua franca: The rise and fall of world languages*. London: Penguin Books.

Spolsky, Bernard. 2004. *Language policy*. Cambridge: Cambridge University Press.

Spolsky, Bernard. 1991. "Hebrew language revitalization within a general theory of second language learning." In *The influence of language on culture and thought: Essays in honor of Joshua A. Fishman's sixty-fifth birthday*, edited by B. Spolsky and R. L. Cooper (137–156). Berlin and New York: Mouton de Gruyter.

Steinhauser, Gabriele. 2016. "English loses currency as Europe's lingua franca after Brexit vote." *The Wall Street Journal*, 27 June. www.wsj.com/articles/eu-to-say-au-revoir-tschuss-to-english-language-1467036600.

Stolton, Samuel. 2018. "Juncker: We are not 'under the rule' of English." *EURACTIV*, 18 September. www.euractiv.com/section/english-language/news/juncker-we-are-not-under-the-rule-of-english/.

Conclusions

This book takes us through some of the defining moments in European language policy, including the drafting and reforms of the European Charter for Regional or Minority Languages (ECRML) (Chapter 1); the development of the multilingualism portfolio in the European Commission (Chapter 2); as well as the growing dominance of English across EU institutions, bodies and agencies (Chapter 3). The controversial issue of EU migrant and non-territorial languages also features prominently (Chapter 4), particularly in the context of a need (or lack thereof) for official EU status for additional languages (Chapter 5). We close with an appraisal of another potentially defining moment in EU language policy, namely Ireland's renewed linguistic and diplomatic landscape in the wake of Brexit (Chapter 6).

The future of European language policy has yet to be written. There is no indication from within the Commission that language policy will play a more significant role in the bloc, as evidenced in the interview with Ó Riain and in Leal's interview with the Commission's Directorate-General for Translation (DGT), the current legal custodians of multilingualism in the EU (Leal 2021, 207–214). In fact, the systematic downgrading of the multilingualism portfolio suggests a *diminished* role for language policy. At the same time, the number and prominence of proposals in the language area within the recent Conference on the future of Europe, along with repeated calls for more qualified majority voting to improve decision-making, suggest a will and a possible means to enhance the role of language policy in the EU.

Moreover, the efforts to reform the ECRML, coupled with Portugal's signature after a 16-year hiatus since the signatures of

DOI: 10.4324/9781003342069-7

Conclusions 147

Table 7.1 The Future of language policy in the EU: Recommendations

1	Create an EU Agency for Linguistic Diversity/ALD within DGT
2	Examine the feasibility of the most popular language policy ideas from the Conference on the future of Europe
3	Study the potential role of a planned language, such as Esperanto, in strengthening the EU's linguistic diversity and organise pilot training in this language for current EU translators and interpreters
4	Implement the measures put forth within the language turn
5	Implement the measures put forth within the translation turn
6	Implement the measures put forth within the transcultural turn

Serbia and Bosnia and Herzegovina, are reason for careful optimism. Ireland's post-Brexit attitude towards multilingualism, encapsulated in the creation of Ó Riain's new post and in the coordinated efforts to forge closer ties with continental Europe, fuel this optimism.

There is enough academic consensus that a *laissez-faire* attitude in the realm of language leads to injustice and unfavourable outcomes – both symbolic and economic – which can only be avoided through overt language policies. The enactment of EU-wide language policies, in turn, can be controversial – because this issue is tied to notions of nationhood and sovereignty, because the EU's jurisdiction is limited in this area, and because a centralised, homogenising force in the realm of language would be undesirable.

However, if the present no-policy drift is allowed to continue, the outlook for vulnerable linguistic communities is uncertain, as is the outlook for the English language as the EU's current lingua franca of sorts. The broader questions are (1) whether the EU will address the "identity crisis" and the "democratic deficit" and, if so, (2) whether it will at long last acknowledge the key part played by language in both. Does the EU wish to deal with citizens, or only with consumers?

In this context, we have arrived at the set of recommendations in Table 7.1 above, which we kept short, concrete and feasible to try and steer EU language policy towards a fairer, more diverse future. That would be in the spirit of the EU's motto, "united in diversity."

Measure 1 is hierarchically above the other five, as it constitutes a pre-requisite for them. As noted repeatedly in previous chapters, the most urgent step to advance language policy and planning is the creation of a unit devoted to it. To placate legal and budgetary concerns, the unit – which we propose to name Agency for Linguistic Diversity (ALD) – should remain within DGT. It would rely on the already existing antennae in each Commission Representation in the member states but would recruit the necessary language policy expertise.

As DGT already has a legal remit in language policy-making, the ALD would merely allow it to exercise this right and duty. Monitoring language policies, practices, ideologies and discourse in the member states would be the main task of the antennae in the Commission Representations, and this would include the measures outlined in the threefold turn proposed for the EU in this book and in Leal (2021). The DGT unit, in turn, would coordinate this pluricentric agency and arbitrate the issues that arise in linguistic diversity in the spirit of EU primary law in this area (see Table 3.1). All ALD staff should have expertise in language policy and planning, as well as reflect the plurality of voices that constitute the debate around linguistic diversity in the EU today. To ensure that ALD actions are not at odds with the state-of-the-art in the relevant academic disciplines, it should comprise a scientific committee with representatives of different disciplines (at least applied linguistics, sociolinguistics, anthropological linguistics, translation and interpreting studies, political theory, philosophy of language and political philosophy).

The ALD would then be tasked with recommendations 2 to 6 in Table 7.1 through pluricentric working groups. Recommendations 2 and 3 should be implemented within a six-month period and yield reports, possibly including proposals for legal acts, to be sent to the Commission and the Parliament for mandatory consideration. Particularly the second part of recommendation 3, pertaining to the pilot-training of translators and interpreters in a planned language such as Esperanto, should lead to clear, evidence-based policy recommendations, and avoid the kind of inaccurate *a priori* conclusions which have bedevilled this area for far too long. Recommendations 2 and 3, which aim for innovative and improved language learning in cooperation with national authorities, stem from proposals at the recent Conference on the future of Europe,[1] and have found a place in a recent report by experts to the European Parliament.[2]

Recommendations 4, 5 and 6 should be staggered across a 10-year period, with the possibility of renewing and recalibrating their objectives for a second 10-year period. Given their scope and complexity, many of the steps outlined within the threefold turn require coordinated efforts across the institutions, bodies and agencies, hence the need for a generous timeframe. As evidenced in this book, the turns are predicated on a *renewed* language mentality, which in turn reflects *existing* language policies, discourse and – to a lesser but still significant extent – ideologies. Thus, they foster the translation of these favourable language policies, discourse and ideologies into language practices; they engender, in short, a multilingual *modus operandi*. Yet transformed language practices do not come about as a result of top-down language policies, as already noted. Therefore, the implementation of recommendations 4 to 6 require coordinated top-down and bottom-up, piecemeal initiatives that will not yield fruits overnight.

These six recommendations do not require treaty change nor significant budget increases. What they do require is political will and better coordination between policy-makers and academia.

Notes

1 See "The EU needs improved language learning" (Conference on the future of Europe - https://futureu.europa.eu/en/processes/Education/f/36/proposals/23893, last accessed in February 2023).
2 See "The European Union's approach to multilingualism in its own communications policy," especially pp. 84–85 (*www.europarl.europa.eu/RegData/etudes/STUD/2022/699648/IPOL_STU(2022)699648_EN.pdf*, last accessed in February 2023).

Reference

Leal, Alice. 2021. *English and translation in the European Union: Unity and multiplicity in the wake of Brexit*. Abingdon & New York: Routledge.

Index

Note: Page numbers in *italic* refers to Tables. Endnotes are indicated by the page number followed by "n" and the note number e.g., 88n1 refers to note 1 on page 88.

Afrikaans 23
Ahrweiler, Hélène 46
allochthonous languages 23, 94–5
Ancient Greek viii, 83
Arabic 8, 23–4, 77, 84, 93–4, 112–13, 125n3, 134
Argentina vii
Asselborn, Jean 122
Auld, William 84
Australia vii, x, xvi, 14, 88n1, 115, 134, 137–8
Austria vii, ix, xiii, 2, 7–10, 14, 32, 81, 95, 117, 119–21, 126
autochthonous languages 3, 16, 94–5, 97, 99

Balibar, Étienne 97, 106, 110
Barroso, José Manuel 31–3, 36, 40
Basque 8, 15–17, 77, 93, 113, 119, 123–4
Belgium vii, 2, 7, 12, 17, 42, 93, 95, 140
Bible 20
Blanke, Detlev 83
Bolivia 143
Bonotti, Matteo 131
Bosnia and Herzegovina 2, 6–11, 111, 146
Brazil 78, 85, 88–9n1, 139

Brexit (UK's withdrawal from the EU) ix, xii, xv, 65, 67, 109, 122–3, 126n7, 129–32, 137–40, 144, 146–7
Broccatelli, Umberto 42
Bulgaria 2, 7–8, 12, 17, 33, 38, 40, 57, 93, 95
Buzek, Jerzy 42

Cameron, David 20
Campbell, Gregory 19
Canada 2, 93n1
Catalan, Catalonia 8, 13, 17, 58, 77, 93–4, 109, 115, 118–20
Cerquiglini, Bernard 23
China, Chinese xi, 16, 65–6, 78, 82–3, 93, 134
citizen participation 52; *see also* civic participation
citizenship 46, 92, 96–7, 105–6
civic participation 34–5; *see also* citizen participation
Cogo, Alessia 64, 131
Columbanus 140
Comité Ad Hoc pour les Langues Régionales (CAHLR) 1
Common Gaelic 20

Index 151

Conference on the future of Europe (2021-2022) xi, 15, 51–2, 98, 111, 146–9, 149n1
conferral (principle of) 46
Conradh na Gaeilge (The Gaelic League) 125n2
constitutional treaty 41
convention 1, 14–16, 18, 21
costs of language services 111
Council of ministers of the European Union (EU Council) vii, x, 43, 77, 119
Council of Europe (CoE) vii, ix, 1–2, 12–14, 99
Croatia, Croatian 2–3, 7–10, 22, 38, 57, 69, 93, 95, 123
Crystal, David 25
culture ix, 5, 21, 31–3, 37, 46–7, 49–52, 54n7, 75, 79, 83–5, 98, 115, 131, 139, 143
Cyprus 2, 7–8, 11, 32, 95, 118, 120, 123

Dahl, Robert 67
Dahrendorf, Ralf 26, 113–14
Dalmatian 123
de Bhaldraithe, Tomás 116
Dell'Alba Report 43, 50
Delors, Jacques 32
democracy 67–8
democratic deficit 52, 97, 106, 147
Derrida, Jacques 67, 96
De Swaan, Abram 31
Deutsch, Karl 49, 67
DGT Info 36, 72
diglossia 113–14, 125n4
Directorate-General for Translation of the European Commission (DGT) vii, x, 12–14, 32, 35–7, 40, 48–9, 54n6, 57, 62, 69, 72, 76, 80, 84, 88, 96, 116, 120, 122, 146, 148
discrimination 27, 78, 99–100
Dublin vii, ix, 126n5, 134, 137, 139, 144n1
Dúchas 21

education viii, xi, 4–5, 25–6, 31–3, 37, 42, 44, 47, 51–2, 54n7, 71, 79, 87, 94, 98–9, 102, 113, 116, 121, 124, 125–6n4, 137, 141
English viii–xi, xv, 12, 14, 19, 21–2, 25–6, 37, 39–40, 52–3, 57–9, 61–2, 64–9, 72–85, 87–9, 92, 93, 101–4, 106, 109, 112–14, 116–23, 125–6, 129–34, 136–40, 142–3, 146–7; American English 131; *English and translation in the European Union* vii, xiii; ELF (English as a lingua franca) xiii–xiv, 53, 57, 59, 63–6, 68, 73–6, 122, 131, 138, 147; *English-only Europe?* 62, 75, 138; *Euro-English* 64, 75, 131, 138; expanding circle 88, 88–9n1; inner circle 64, 103, 88n1, 131; outer circle 64, 88–9n1, 131; post-Brexit role 122; ubiquity in diplomacy 134, 137–40; World Englishes 64, 130
Esperanto x–xi, 20, 33–4, 36–45, 50–1, 76–9, 81–7, 99–100, 103, 105, 124, 147–8; cultural value 43, 45, 50; native speakers 44, 65; origins 82–4; unique grammatical system 86
Estonia 2, 7, 12, 17, 95
Eurobarometer 27, 68, 105
Europe viii, xi–xii, xiv, xvi, 1, 3, 12–13, 15, 19, 21–4, 27, 33, 36–7, 39–42, 50–2, 68, 72, 76, 85, 92–4, 98, 101–2, 111, 115, 118, 131, 138, 140, 143, 147, 149n1–2; citizen identification 27–8; European identity 28, 36, 46, 67–8, 76, 110, 115, 122
European anthem 42–4, 77
European Bureau for Less-Used Languages (EBLUL) x, xiin1, xiv
European Charter on Regional and Minority Languages (ECRML) x, xiv–xv, 1–2, 3–8, 10–13, 15–17, 21–4, 26–7, 46, 92–4, 99, 124, 146

European Citizens' Initiative
(ECI) 34–5, 41–2, 44, 52
European Civil Society Platform
for Multilingualism (ECSPM)
33, 37, 39, 41–2
European Coal and Steel
Community 45, 109
European Commission xiii,
13, 27–8, 31–2, 34–5, 37,
41–3, 45, 53, 57, 59, 62–3, 73,
87–8, 92, 94, 98, 105, 131,
142–3, 146; *Communication on
Multilingualism* (2009) 37; DGT
(*see* Directorate-General for
Translation of the European
Commission (DGT)); procedural
languages 62–3, 119; SurveyLang
2012 (*see* SurveyLang2012)
European Council 6, 12
European Court of Justice (Court
of Justice of the EU) 34, 77
European Economic Community
(EEC) 40, 58, 119
European Esperanto Union
(EEU) 41–2
European Parliament xii, 34–5,
41–5, 48, 50–1, 63, 77, 118, 123,
148
European Union vii, xii–xiii, 12,
31, 35, 47–8, 50–2, 57–8, 76, 92,
97, 115, 118–19, 149n2; anti-EU
movements 132; competence,
areas of 45–8, 61, 70–1, 98–9,
103, 109, 114–15, 121, 142; Irish
Presidency vii, x, 126; language
policy vii–viii, xiii–xvi, 12, 25,
27, 34, 36, 45–6, 48–9, 52–4n6,
67–8, 70, 76, 81, 85, 88, 94, 98,
105–6, 109–10, 112, 114, 122–5,
133, 135–6, 138, 141, 143,
146–8; EU Agency for
Linguistic Diversity/ALD 147;
less-used languages x, xiin1, 13,
17, 112; official languages xi, 3,
12, 19, 25–6, 40, 42, 58–9, 62,
69–70, 73, 77–8, 88n1, 92, 101,
105, 111–12, 114–16, 118–20,
123–5, 133; shared destiny 45,
109–10; translation regimes
62–3; working languages 12,
57–8, 63, 73, 77, 92, 97, 116,
119–20, 137

Faye, Jean-Pierre 68
Ferguson, Charles A. 113
Figeľ, Ján 31–2
Fishman, Joshua A. 24, 96, 113
France, French vii, ix–x, 2, 7–8,
12, 14–15, 17–18, 20, 22–4, 39,
39–42, 49, 57–8, 62–3, 66, 69,
72–5, 77–83, 86, 88, 93–4, 109,
113, 117, 119–20, 123, 126n7,
132–41
Francophonie 23, 73, 137–8, 141
Frank, Helmar 78

Gaelic *see* Scottish Gaelic
Gaeltacht ix, 141
Gardner, Jeremy 64, 130
German, Germany vii, x, 2, 7–10,
12, 17, 21, 24, 36, 40, 42, 57–8,
62–3, 69, 72–3, 76, 78, 81–3, 87,
93, 95, 109, 119–22, 132–4
Good Friday Agreement 97, 101
Greece 2, 7, 12, 14–15, 17–18, 95
Greek (Ancient) viii, 8, 15, 18, 57,
62, 67, 83, 93
Grimm, Dieter 49, 67
Grin, François: 52, 63, 87, 101–3,
105, 111, 125, 130; Grin report
(2005) 136

Habermas, Jürgen 49, 67
Hahn, Johannes 32
Handzlik, Małgorzata 44
Hebrew x, 82–3, 93, 142
Heidegger, Martin 110
Henry VIII ix
Herder, Johann G. 66
Hiberno-English viii
Hijmans, Alex 139
Hübner, Danuta 119, 123
human rights 2, 25, 67–8
Humboldt, Wilhelm von 66
Hungary, Hungarian 2, 3, 7–10,
32, 57, 68, 82, 93, 95, 111

Index 153

identity viii, 28, 36, 46, 50, 65–8, 76, 79, 97–8, 110, 115, 122, 131, 141, 147
iMeasc 139
Indo-European 82
integration xi–xii, 24, 35–6, 40–1, 49, 76–7, 92, 98, 101, 115
intercomprehension 61, 69–71, 79, 81, 85, 87–8, 103, 124, 138, 142
Ireland vii–ix, xv, 2, 4, 6–9, 12, 17, 19–20, 39–41, 53, 58, 69, 84, 88n1, 95, 98, 100–1, 105, 111, 113, 115, 117–19, 125n2, 125–6n4, 126n5, 129–44, 132, 137, 144n1, 146–7; Department of Foreign Affairs (Foreign Ministry) vii, ix, 120–1, 129, 132, 137, 140–1; Irish diplomatic service 129, 132, 134; National University of Ireland 144n1; Official Languages Acts (2003 and 2021) 115
Irish language vii–x, 19, 38, 58, 69, 72, 98, 111, 113, 116, 135, 139, 142; EU official status 97, 112, 115
Islam 68
Israel 80, 112, 125n3, 142
Italian 8, 12, 20, 40, 42–3, 57–8, 61, 81, 83, 93, 97; Italy 2, 7, 12, 17, 20, 40, 42, 78, 93, 95, 119, 123, 140

Jenkins, Jennifer 65, 131
Jewish 82–3, 125n3
Junker, Jean-Claude 31–2, 131

Kachru, Braj 64, 88–9
Kaye, Paul xiii, 143
Killilea Resolution 12
Kinnock, Neil 45
Kraus, Peter A. 23, 26, 46, 49–50, 54n3, 76, 113, 141
Kurdish 9, 18, 20
Kymlicka, Will 24–5, 141

La infana raso 84
Lacordaire, Henri 126

language: agglutinative 82; isolating 82
language-as-problem 25–7
language-as-resource 26–7
language-as-right 25–6
language learning xi, 33, 36–8, 42, 51, 65, 87, 100, 102, 112, 142, 149n1; propaedeutic method 10, 39
language policy vii–viii, xii–xvi, 12, 25, 27, 34, 36, 45–6, 48–9, 52–4, 54n6, 57–8, 70, 76, 81, 85, 88, 94, 96, 98, 105–6, 109–26, 133, 135–6, 138, 141, 143, 146–8; common language xii, 49, 62, 66–8, 76, 78, 85, 105, 122; *laissez-faire* 88, 126n7, 147; language use 25, 64, 70, 95, 113, 133, 142; neutral language 31, 42–3, 51, 65, 78, 81, 83, 92, 99–100; official status 19, 97, 112, 115–16, 120, 122–3, 129
language turn 69–70, 79, 141, 147
Latin viii, 42, 77, 83, 87, 140
Le Monde 15
Letta, Enrico 121
ligatures *see* options and ligatures
lingua franca xiii–xiv, 53, 57–88, 104–5, 122, 124, 131–2, 138, 147
linguistic diversity vii, x, 12, 19, 25, 33–5, 50, 58, 77, 104–5, 147–8
linguistic (in)justice xiv, 88, 101, 103–4, 141
Lisbon (Treaty of) 110

Maastricht, Treaty of 27, 46
Mac Eoin, Gearóid ix
Mac Giolla Chríost, Diarmait 131
Malta 2, 7, 12, 17, 22, 95; Maltese 57–8, 62, 93, 97
maxi-min principle 61, 84–5, 124–5
McKenna, Patricia 44
migrant and non-territorial languages xv, 16, 22–7, 85, 92–106
migrants 3, 16, 23–4, 96, 100

Index

Mill, John Stuart 49, 67
MIME project (Mobility and inclusion in multilingual Europe) 52
minority languages 1–28, 51, 92–3, 104, 109, 116, 118, 146; four dimensions in the EU 93
Minority SafePack (ECI) 34–5, 41–2, 44, 48, 52
Mirandés 6, 77, 93, 123–4
Mitterrand, François 15
Modiano, Marko 64–5, 130–1
Monnet, Jean 46
monolingualism 12, 20, 22, 25, 33, 40, 85
multilingualism vii, xii–xvii, 1, 22, 25–6, 31–54, 62, 64, 68–72, 77–9, 84–5, 87, 97, 103–5, 109, 112, 114, 122, 125–6, 129–44, 146–7
Multilingualism accelerator (MLA) 33–4, 38–9
Munduruku, Daniel 89n2

NATO 67, 76
Navracsics, Tibor 32
Nic Craith, Máiréad 22–4, 27, 92
non-discrimination *see* discrimination
Novak, Ludmila 44
Nynorsk 14

Öffentlichkeit 49, 67; *see also* public sphere
Ó Huiginn, Seán 100
Old Testament 83
Ó Murchú, Máirtín vii
options and ligatures 26, 113–14, 124, 140–2, 144n1
Orban, Leonard 32, 36, 40, 48
Ó Riagáin, Dónall 13, 18–19
Ottoman Empire 18

Pakistani 16
Panella, Marco 42
pandemic (Coronavirus) xvi, 110, 121

parity of esteem 92, 97–8, 100, 105, 122, 131
Pei, Mario 83
Pereira, Anabela 36
Phillipson, Robert 45, 62–3, 75, 87, 113, 138
Piron, Claude 44
Poland vii, x, 2, 7–12, 68, 74, 82, 85, 95, 123, 133, 136; Polish viii, 9, 20, 42, 44, 57, 74, 82–3, 119, 123, 133, 136, 139
Portugal 2, 6–7, 12, 17, 22, 54n8, 95, 123, 146; Portuguese 24, 36, 40, 57, 61, 79, 83, 93, 134
propaedeutical approach xi
proportionality (principle of) 46, 48, 54n4
public sphere 49, 67–8; *see also* Öffentlichkeit

Québec vii

recommendation 1, 11, 14–15, 18, 21, 42–3, 148
Ringe, Nils 22, 68, 85
Roma 9, 27, 99; Romani 3, 9, 11, 93–4
Romania 2, 7–10, 22, 32–3, 36, 95
Ruiz, Richard 25–6
rule of law 67–8
Russia 17, 111; Russian 7, 9, 20, 79–82, 83, 93, 134

Saint Gall/Sankt Gallen 140
Sámi 3, 8–10, 93–4
Sapir-Whorf (hypothesis) 66
Schottenstift 140
Scotland 19–20, 140
Scottish Gaelic viii, ix, 9, 10, 17, 20
Scotus 140
Seidlhofer, Barbara 64–5
Selten, Reinhard 42
Serbia 2, 7, 81, 111, 146; Serbian 10, 81, 93, 123
Shakespeare 83, 88n1
shared fate 110–11, 121–2
Sign languages 3, 93–4, 101, 104, 106n1

Single European Act 41
Slovenia 2, 7–11, 38, 95
South Africa 85
Soviet Union 44
Spain 2, 7–10, 93n2, 95, 119–21, 123, 139–40; Spanish 17, 24, 42, 57, 61, 72, 81, 83, 93, 118–21, 132, 134, 140
Spolsky, Bernard 25–7, 113, 142
Springboard to languages (S2L) 33, 37–8, 42
Statutes of Kilkenny ix
subsidiarity (principle of) 46, 48, 54n3
SurveyLang 2012, 10
Sweden 2, 3, 7–10, 22, 95; Swedish 10–11, 40, 57, 72–3, 93
Syria 24

Tamazight (Berber) 93
Tišljar, Zlatko 38
transcultural competence 70–1
transcultural turn 69, 79, 147
translation: translation turn 69, 71, 79, 147
Trump, Donald 121
Turkey 14–18, 20, 111, 120; Turkish 10, 15–16, 18, 77, 82, 84, 93, 118, 120, 122–3

Ukraine 2, 7–11, 15, 111
United Kingdom 2, 6–10, 14
United Nations (UN) 7, 80, 134
unity (versus multiplicity) 114
USA 45, 67, 131–2

van Gunsteren, Herman 110
Van Parijs, Philippe 53, 61, 84, 103–4, 124
Vassiliou, Androulla 32, 37
Vienna vii, ix, xiii–xiv, 80, 83, 117–18, 135, 140
Vietnamese 82, 134
Von der Leyen, Ursula 32, 73

Weber, Max 113
Welsh ix, 10, 14, 17–18
Western Europe 13
Wild Geese/*oies sauvages* 140
Williams, Melissa 110
Wright, Sue 49, 59, 61

Yeats, Gráinne 135
Yeats, Micheál 135
Yeats, W. B. 135
Yiddish 10, 83–4, 93
Yugoslavia (former) 23

Zamenhof, L. L. 82–4

For Product Safety Concerns and Information please contact our EU representative GPSR@taylorandfrancis.com
Taylor & Francis Verlag GmbH, Kaufingerstraße 24, 80331 München, Germany

www.ingramcontent.com/pod-product-compliance
Lightning Source LLC
Chambersburg PA
CBHW051746230426
43670CB00012B/2185